501 Little-Known Facts, Obscure Trivia, World Records and Historical Minutia from the State of Mississippi

To: Dink,
Enjoy the read.
Merry Christmas 2012

D.K. White

By D.K. White

NAUTILUS PUBLISHING
Taylor, Mississippi

For bulk orders and educational discounts, contact:
    The Nautilus Publishing Company
    One Town Square Lane, Suite 5
    Post Office Box 40
    Taylor, MS 38673
    Tel: 662-513-0159
    Fax: 662-234-9266
    www.nautiluspublishing.com
    info@nautiluspublishing.com

White, D.K. (1956-   )
    501 Little-Know Facts, Obscure Trivia, World Records & Historical Minutia
    about the State of Mississippi —1st ed.
    ISBN # 978-1-936946-10-5

Cover design by Le'Herman Payton

The author and publisher welcome feedback and contributions to future editions.
To contact the author, visit www.*501trivia.com*

PRINTED IN CANADA
through a partnership with Friesens Printing

10   9   8   7   6   5   4   3   2   1

CONTENTS

CELEBRITY & ENTERTAINMENT

Tammy Wynette was born and raised in Itawamba Co. near Tremont. Her real name was Virginia Wynette Pugh. She was married to five different men (George Jones being the only entertainer among them). Ironically, two of her biggest hits were: "D-I-V-O-R-C-E" and "Stand by Your Man."

Sam Cooke, the hit-maker who brought the world "Chain Gang," "Twistin' the Night Away," "Cupid," and "You Send Me" was born in Clarksdale.

County music legend Conway Twitty was born in Friars Point in 1933. His real name was Harold Jenkins, but a promoter urged him to change it. Harold looked at a map of the South and noticed the towns Conway, Arkansas and Twitty, Texas. Twitty had fifty-five #1 hits—more than any other performer in any genre.

Johnny Cash was arrested in Starkville in 1965 for public drunkenness (though Cash claimed he was jailed for picking flowers at 2:00 a.m.). He later wrote a song about the incident, "Starkville City Jail."

Lynard Skynyrd's plane crashed outside of Gillsburg, just south of McComb in 1977 when it ran out of gas. Six of the 26 passengers lost their lives, including three band members.

In 1944 Chickasaw Co. witnessed the birth of Bobbie Gentry. She sang the 1967 hit "Ode to Billy Joe." In a *Life* magazine photo after her rise to stardom, Gentry strolls across a bridge over the Tallahatchie River. She claimed she never had a particular bridge in mind, of the many that cross the river, when she wrote the song.

Dr. Hook, of the rock-n-roll band "Dr. Hook and the Medicine Show," was really George Cummings from Meridian. The band's biggest hit came in 1972 — "Cover of the Rolling Stone." The words of the song detailed how a band knew they'd made it to the Big Time when featured on the cover. *Rolling Stone*, showing some humor, put the band on the cover, but they used caricatures of band members instead of a photograph.

Hollywood first came to Mississippi in 1920 with the production of the silent film, *Heart of Maryland*. Natchez was used as the backdrop.

Oxford's William Faulkner's great-grandfather, William Falkner, also wrote. He had a bestselling book titled "The White Rose of Memphis." The younger William added the "u" to his last name in 1918 to dress it up when attempting to join the British Royal Air Force.

————

"The Commodores" had a string of hits in the 1970s. Okolona native Milan "Bunny" Williams played keyboard for the group.

————

"The Allman Brothers" had a few hits in the 1970s, too. Drumming on their albums was John Lee Johnson from Ocean Springs.

————

Legions of Parrotheads know singer/songwriter Jimmy Buffett was born in Pascagoula (his nickname back then was Bubba). But many don't know that Buffet is one of only nine authors in the history of the New York Times bestseller list to have reached number one on both the fiction and nonfiction lists.

————

William Faulkner's last book published was in 1963, *The Reivers*. In 1969 Hollywood made it into a movie starring Steve McQueen. McQueen's character "borrowed" his employer's car and took it to Memphis. The actual word "reiver" is old Scottish slang for horse or cattle thief.

————

Long before casinos brought big name entertainers to Mississippi, Gus Stevens' Supper Club was doing the same thing. Johnny Rivers sang at the club, as did Mel Torme, Jerry Lee Lewis and Jayne Mansfield. Andy Griffith, Justin Wilson and Brother Dave Gardner all performed comedy acts, too.

————

Actress Stella Stevens, who starred in *The Poseidon Adventure, Girls, Girls, Girls* (with Elvis), and the original *The Nutty Professor,* was born in Yazoo City.

————

A short detour off of Highway 49, just north of Mendenhall, is D'Lo Water Park. Movie buffs may recognize the rocky rapids from the Sirens Scene in the Cohen Brothers film *O Brother, Where art Thou?*

————

More than 95% of the movie *The Help* was filmed in Mississippi. The film has grossed more than $200 million. The film's director, Jackson native Tate Taylor, and the cast have won more than 65 awards.

Neil Simon's hit play "Biloxi Blues" was adapted for the screen in 1988. Observant moviegoers will readily know the movie was not filmed in Mississippi. In an early scene, soldiers are standing at attention on the Biloxi base grounds—in the background is a mountain range.

Film and television star Dana Andrews was born in Collins in 1909. Mr. Andrews listed 65 films to his credit.

Laurel native Ray Walston will be remembered by several generations. For more mature Mississippians, Walston will always be Our Favorite Martian. For a younger set, he'll be "Mr. Hand" from *Fast Times at Ridgemont High.*

Elvis was born a twin. The brother was stillborn. An only child, Elvis was pampered by his mother. Elvis cut his first record as a gift for his mother's birthday. His total record sales are estimated over one billion with 40% of those international sales. He starred in 33 movies, too.

In Oxford, William Faulkner's last home, Rowan Oak, was built before the Civil War. When the author purchased the property in 1930, it was known as "The Bailey Place." He lived there until his death in 1962. Ten years later, his daughter Jill, sold Rowan Oak to the University of Mississippi.

Young Elvis Presley earned some of that soulful blues sound the hard way. When he was a child in Tupelo, Elvis' father did a short stint in Parchman after being convicted of stealing hogs.

Buffalo Bill Cody's fame was in great part due to the dime novels about his exploits and adventures. The author of those books was Adams County native Colonel Prentiss Ingraham, who wrote more than 200 Buffalo Bill stories. Ingraham died in 1904. As a former Rebel soldier, he was buried in Beauvoir's Confederate Cemetery.

Philadelphia native and country music start Marty Stuart owns the world's largest private collection of country music memorabilia.

Mississippi Delta native Lawrence Gordon produced the films *48 Hours, Predator, Die Hard, Field of Dreams, Point Break,* and dozens of other Hollywood hits. In the 1980s, he also served as president of 20th Century Fox.

A resident of Nesbit, Mississippi, rock-n-roll legend Jerry Lee Lewis was raised in Ferriday, Louisiana, just across the river from Natchez. His sister turned their old homestead into a shrine to The Killer. Today, she still operates The Jerry Lee Lewis Museum...and Liquor Store.

More famous today as the Sucarnochee Revue, a television show featuring musicians from the Black Belt of Mississippi and Alabama, there is also town by that name. Located on Highway 45 in Kemper County, the town was founded in 1870 and is Native Mississippian for "place where hogs fatten."

Time and CNN called Kosciusko native Oprah Winfrey "arguably the most powerful woman in the world." *Forbes* magazine named her the first African-American female billionaire—quite a rise from a childhood on a Mississippi farm without indoor plumbing.

Two Mississippi natives are the most sought-after narrators for documentary films and television commercials — Charleston native Morgan Freeman and Arkabutla native James Earl Jones. Back in the days of the CB radio craze, Jones's handle was "Darth Vader."

Leland native Jim Henson created The Muppets. He responded to those who asked that he'd had two close friends growing up, both named Kermit. Of all his puppets, Kermit the Frog was his favorite due to its small size and light weight that would not tire his arm when performing.

After her historic debut at The Metropolitan Opera, Leontyne Price received a 42-minute ovation — the longest in Met history. She was the first African-American to earn the "top fee" salary at the Met.

Biloxi native David Sheffield mailed unsolicited comedy sketches to Saturday Night Live. His work was so impressive, the producers hired him full-time in 1980. As the new hire, Sheffield chose to work with the newest, youngest cast member — a 19-year-old kid named Eddie Murphy. Sheffield became Murphy's go to scriptwriter. His credits include *Coming to America*, *The Nutty Professor*, and *Boomerang*. Sheffield's films have grossed over a billion dollars.

Biloxi's Mary Ann Mobley was crowned Miss America in 1959. Her sorority sister, Natchez native Lynda Lee Mead, won the crown in 1960.

Amory native Sam Haskell was the long-time Worldwide Head of Television for The William Morris Agency. Haskell, considered to be on of the most powerful men in entertainment, was instrumental in launching *The Cosby Show*, *The Fresh Prince of Bel Air*, *Who Wants to be a Millionaire*, *Everybody Loves Raymond*, and *Lost*.

———

The new "Benji" was a homeless stray found in Pass Christian.

———

Sledge native Charley Pride was passed off as a white singer for two years after the hit record, "Just Between You and Me." Pride had 39 #1 country hits. He is still the only African-American to be inducted into the Grand Ole Opry. Before he could rely on his singing talent for a living, Charley was a professional baseball player.

———

Hazelhurst native Robert Leroy Johnson has been called "the most important blues singer that ever lived." He reportedly achieved his greatness by selling his soul to the devil at the crossroads.

———

Clarksdale native Ike Turner co-wrote what was very likely the first rock and roll hit record, *Rocket 88*. As a talent scout he found a gifted singer named Annie Mae Bullock. He made Bullock part of his act, as well as part of his life. Bullock's stage name is Tina Turner.

———

Meridian native Jimmie "The Singing Brakeman" Rodgers is the only performer to be inducted into all four major music Halls of Fame and was the very first member of the Country Music Hall of Fame.

———

Pontotoc's Delaney Bramlett is credited with teaching the Beatles' George Harrison how to play the slide guitar. He also had an influence on the guitar playing of Eric Clapton.

———

Robin Roberts, born and raised in Pass Christian, is co-anchor of ABC's "Good Morning America." Before her ESPN career, she had been a prolific scorer on the Lady Lions of Southeast Louisiana University's basketball team. Her father was one of the Tuskegee Airmen.

———

Author John Grisham has an undergraduate degree from MSU and is a law school grad of Ole Miss. Before becoming a full-time writer, he served in the legislature as a state representative. Five years after his first book, *A Time to Kill*, was published, he went back, tried a case, and won the trial.

Milton Babbitt, raised in Jackson, was awarded a Pulitzer Prize in 1982 for "his life's work as a distinguished and seminal American composer." Babbit's students at Julliard included Stephen Sondheim.

———

Faith Hill was born in 1967 in Jackson, but grew up down Hwy 49 in Star as an adopted child. She claims that seeing Elvis perform in Jackson, around 1976, deeply influenced her choice to pursue a musical career.

Calvin Broadus has deep Mississippi roots even though he was born in Los Angeles. Both his parents are natives of our Pike County. Calvin's professional stage name is more recognizable…Snoop Dogg.

———

The band "3 Doors Down" was formed in Escatawpa in 1994. Their debut album in 2000 went platinum six times, topping six million copies sold.

———

Holly Springs native Shepard Smith is one of America's top television news anchors.

———

DISASTERS

A 1936 tornado in Tupelo killed 216 residents and injured nearly 700.

———

Over 3,000 Mississippians died in the Yellow Fever Epidemic of 1877. During another outbreak in 1899, pre-cure physicians claimed the disease had entered the state on imported bananas.

———

From 1880 to 2003, Mississippi had three of the top ten counties nationally with F-3 and above tornado strikes. Union County has the dubious #1 spot with Simpson County ranked 2nd and Jasper County in 6th place among the total 3,141 counties in the U.S.

———

The 1811 Great New Madrid Earthquake is well-known, but the state of Mississippi has been hit since. In 1931 a quake caused minor damage, mostly toppling chimneys, in Belzoni, Tillatoba, Water Valley, and Charleston. In 1955, a tremor was reported from Biloxi to Bay St. Louis. And in 1967 an earthquake centered near Greenville registered 3.8 on the Richter Scale.

———

The only U.S. nuclear bomb tests east of the Mississippi River took place in Lamar County in 1964 and 1966. Both blasts were underground in the Tatum Salt Dome, approximately 30 miles southwest of Hattiesburg. The first (and larger) blast was equal to 5000 tons of TNT. The bomb was detonated 2,700 feet under ground.

———

In 1840, a mile-wide twister came across the Mississippi river and smashed into Natchez and 317 people were killed. It was the second highest death toll from a single tornado in U.S. History.

———

The Mississippi River Flood of 1927 is generally considered the greatest national disaster in U.S. history. The National Safety Council estimated deaths in the Yazoo-Mississippi Delta at 1,000. The flood directly affected 185,495 Mississippians. 41,673 homes were flooded. 21,836 buildings were destroyed. 62,089 buildings were damaged. 6,873 cattle died. 31,740 hogs perished. 266,786 poultry drowned. The entire Delta crop was lost.

———

A Confederate troop train derailment is Mississippi's worst railroad accident. At the Chunky River, outside Hickory, in February 1863 forty soldiers died when the train ran off the bridge. It might have been worse if not for quick rescue actions by the nearby First Choctaw Battalion.

In 1940, the Rhythm Night Club caught fire in Natchez and 207 souls were lost, making it the state's worst fire disaster. A careless match tossed on Spanish moss decorations that had been sprayed with an insecticide is believed to have been the source.

The nation's worst maritime disaster originated at Vicksburg. The *Sultana* steamboat was packed with Union soldiers in April 1865. Under strain of carrying seven times her legal passenger limit, the boilers exploded and an estimated 1800 of the 2400 aboard were killed.

One of the worst-ever explosions in Mississippi happened on the River between Clarksdale and Tunica in 1858. The steamboat *Pennsylvania* experienced a boiler explosion resulting in 200 of her 450 passengers and crew either killed or missing and never recovered.

Purvis was ravaged by a deadly twister in 1908 that took 143 lives.

In 2005, Hurricane Katrina killed 235 Mississippians in 13 counties.

1969's Hurricane Camille killed 172.

SPORTS

Notre Dame won the 1977 college football championship with an 11-1 record. The one loss was a 20-13 defeat at the hands of Ole Miss. Junior Joe Montana was the Irish quarterback that season.

———

At Davis Wade Stadium in Sept. 2000, Mississippi State University beat the Florida Gators 47-35. Rex Grossman played quarterback for the Gators and Steve Spurrier was their head coach. The Bulldog victory was significant because it ended Florida's 72-game winning streak against un-ranked teams.

———

In 1974 U.S.M. was doing major renovations to M.M. Roberts Stadium and, consequently, the football team played all their games on the road. With Jeff Bower at quarterback, they posted a winning 6-5 record.

———

Veterans Memorial Stadium in Jackson no longer hosts SEC Football. For many years the stadium hosted SEC double-headers, as both Ole Miss and Mississippi State played games there. Ole Miss's last SEC game was a win over Arkansas in 1993. Mississippi State's last win there was over LSU in 1990. The Egg Bowl was played in the stadium every season from 1973-1990.

———

Walter Payton had a brother who played in the NFL. Walter's older brother, Eddie, played five seasons in the league. In 1980 he led the NFL in kickoff return yards. The NFL's highest honor—the Man of the Year trophy—is named for Walter.

———

Veterans Memorial Stadium's record for attendance is not from an SEC game. A game between Alcorn State and Mississippi Valley State in 1984 holds the record. Valley's Totten-to-Rice connection was averaging 64 points a game. Alcorn focused on defense and won 42-28.

———

A short list of famous major league baseball players who hail from Mississippi includes Dmitri Young, Frank White, Seth Smith, George Scott, Jay Powell, Roy Oswalt, Julio Borbon, Dave Parker, Barry Lyons, Larry Herndon, Boo Ferris, Chet Lemon, Jake Gibbs, Ellis Burks, Oil Can Boyd, Don Blasingame, and, of course, Dizzy Dean.

———

Canton's L.C. Greenwood was a stalwart of the 1970s Pittsburgh Steelers' "Steel Curtain." He owns four Super Bowl rings and was a 6-time All-Pro.

Olive Branch resident, Ricky Stenhouse, Jr., makes his living on the senior circuit of the NASCAR auto racing association. Lake Speed is our state's best-known NASCAR racer. Speed has one win and 75 top ten finishes over his 19-year career.

The Mississippi Department of Wildlife and Fisheries estimates that 1.5 million deer live inside our state boundaries. Only Texas and Michigan support more deer than Mississippi.

Babe Ruth hit his final two home runs, numbers 713 and 714, off the "Mississippi Mudcat" in 1935. "Mudcat" was Guy Bush from Aberdeen. Bush survived that day and eventually won 176 big league games.

Kiln native Brett Favre did not start off his NFL career with a bang. During his rookie year with the Falcons, he threw exactly four passes — two incomplete and two interceptions. He fared better as a Packer. When Favre retired he held 24 NFL quarterback records, including most career touchdowns, most career passing yards, most career pass completions, and most career victories as a starting quarterback.

Basketball fans from South Mississippi recall the great Wendell Ladner. Coming out of Hancock North Central High School, Ladner had 84 college scholarship offers. Before going pro, Ladner averaged 20 points and 16 rebounds per game at the University of Southern Mississippi. Tragically, he lost his life in a commercial jetliner crash at the age of 26.

Clinton's Larry Myricks won the bronze medal in the Seoul Korea 1988 Olympics with a 27' 1" effort in the long jump. He was 32 years old. A broken foot in 1976 and the 1980 boycott took away chances to compete when he was younger.

As a punter at the University of Southern Mississippi in the early 1970s, Ray Guy averaged almost 45 yards per punt for his college career. He also kicked a then-record 61-yard field goal in 1973 against Utah State. Guy never had a punt returned for a touchdown.

The Big Three state universities have all undergone sports nickname transformations since their early days: The Golden Eagles used to be named the Southerners; the Bulldogs were known as the Maroons; and Ole Miss was called the Flood.

Gulfport's Lem Barney was a perennial All-Pro defensive back for the Detroit Lions from the mid 1960s through the mid 1970s. Motown singer Marvin Gaye once tried out for the team and the two became friends. Barney sang backup in Marvin's great hit "What's Going On." Lem Barney was inducted into the Pro Football Hall of Fame in 1992.

———

Sammy Winder, star running back in the early 1980s for the Denver Broncos was a college walk-on in 1977 at the University of Southern Mississippi. Winder makes his home in Madison, Mississippi.

———

The Bulldog football team is prone to bowl streaks. After losing four bowl games in a row between 1991 and 1998, the Bulldogs have reversed their fortunes. As of 2011, they've won five bowl games in a row.

———

The Great Southern Club on the beach in east Gulfport is officially the state's oldest golf course, hailing from 1910. The original nine holes had crushed oyster shell tee boxes and sand greens. The course hosted the PGA's Gulfport Open and in 1945, Sam Snead beat Byron Nelson in a playoff. The current Pass Christian Isles Golf Course may be older by eight years; however, it ceased to exist for a time and therefore has not been open consecutively, as has the Great Southern.

———

The Ole Miss men's basketball team has had a few shining moments. In 1970, forward Johnny Neumann led the nation in scoring at 40.1 points per game. It ranks fifth all time for the highest season average. Neumann played before the advent of the three-point line.

———

Archie Manning was Senior Class President and Valedictorian at Drew High School. He wasn't always #18 at Ole Miss. His freshman year Manning wore #15.

———

The Golden Eagles football team ended Alabama's 19-year home-campus winning streak in Tuscaloosa. The Eagles beat the Tide 38-29 in 1982. They beat them again, in Birmingham, in 1990 by a score of 27-24.

———

If you were flipping channels in the mid 1980s and caught some professional wrestling, there's a chance you saw Clinton resident, Ted DiBiase. He performed under the nickname the "Million Dollar Man." His signature move was the Sleeper Hold and in keeping with the nickname, after his win, he would stuff a $100 bill into the loser's mouth.

Nick Revon earned All-State Junior College basketball honors in the late 1940s. He was actually in the 11th and 12th grades when he played for Hinds Junior College.

———

Ole Miss's Jake Gibbs is the only Mississippi athlete to earn All-American honors in two sports — football and baseball.

———

The University of Southern Mississippi began having a live "Golden Eagle" at games beginning in 1980. His name is Seymour d'Campus.

———

Wildlife biologists estimate our bobcat population at over 50,000. The beaver population is about 25,000. The ever-growing coyote number is about 40,000. Same goes for alligators. The black bear population is estimated to be between 40 and 50. The official stance of Mississippi is that panthers are extinct. There is a vocal minority that disputes this.

———

Between 2003 and 2008 the South Panola High School football team did not lose a single game — 89 wins in a row. That streak ranks as the third longest, ever, in the country.

———

Way back in 1904, the Ole Miss football team beat Union College 114-0. There have been 73 shellackings worse than that in NCAA history. The all-time leader is Georgia Tech's 222-0 victory over Cumberland in 1916 in which Tech ran for 1,680 yards and did not attempt a single pass.

———

Hattiesburg produced quite a pair of Shorts — the basketball-playing brother combo Eugene and Purvis Short. Purvis played 12 NBA seasons and averaged over 17 per game (including scoring 59 on New Jersey one night in 1984). Older brother Eugene played for Seattle and the Knicks.

———

To say Mississippi State's baseball team has a rich history is an understatement. Bulldog teams have won 16 S.E.C. championships, made 8 appearances at the College World Series, and have made the NCAA tournament 29 times.

———

Ole Miss's Bruiser Kinard once put a kick-off so deep in the end zone, he single-handedly tackled the returner before he reached the goal line. Mississippian Mary Mills was the number one golfer for four years at Millsaps College (on the men's squad). As a pro, she won USGA Women's Open and the LPGA Championship twice.

In today's college basketball world, all the hoopla centers on March Madness — the NCAA tournament — but this wasn't always the case. The NCAA used to only invite conference champs and not many: 16 teams in 1968, for example. This meant the real post-season interest was in the National Invitational Tournament (N.I.T.). The Golden Eagles of Southern won the N.I.T. in 1987.

———

During decade 1950-1959, the Ole Miss football team had the second highest winning percentage among major independents and teams playing in the major conferences. The Rebels won 78% of their games. Many consider the 1959 team one of the best teams in NCAA history. The 1959 squad scored 325 points, while surrendering only 21. Eight of their 11 games ended in shutouts.

———

Modern fans might believe the National Football League's First Family runs through the Mississippi Mannings. But football history buffs know that the First Family of Mississippi Football would have to be the Poole family. Fifteen Poole family members have earned football scholarships to Ole Miss while five have gone on to play in the NFL — including Buster, Ray and Barney.

———

The Mississippi saltwater record for largest fish caught is a Blue Marlin that weighed over 1,054 pounds. There is a tie for the lightest saltwater record; a bonefish and silver perch, both at 4 ounces.

———

For freshwater fishing, the state bass record is 18 pounds, 15 ounces. It was caught in 1992 at Natchez State Park Lake.

———

Mississippi State's Dudy Noble Field/Polk-DeMent Stadium currently holds the NCAA record for the largest single-game, on-campus baseball attendance, at 14,991. It also hosted the largest SEC crowd for a 3-game weekend series at 29,915.

———

College football fans may believe that Natchez native Hugh Green holds Mississippi's best finish for college football's Heisman Trophy. He finished 2nd in 1980. But the 1959 Heisman winner, LSU's Billy Cannon, was originally from Philadelphia, Mississippi.

———

The 1945 Hiesman winner, Army's Doc Blanchard, went to high school at Bay St. Louis' St. Stanislaus.

Starkville native Jerry Rice is generally regarded as the best wide receiver in history. He holds more NFL records — touchdowns, receptions, yards gained — than any other player at any position. The NFL ranked Rice #1 in the greatest players of all time.

Mississippian Eli Manning has twice been named Super Bowl Most Valuable Player.

In a 1969 game against Alabama, Archie Manning threw for 426 yards and ran for another 104. The 540-yard performance is still an SEC record. Ole Miss lost the game 33-32.

Steve McNair still holds the NCAA record for most offensive yards in a career — 16,283 yards rushing and passing.

Laurel native and long jumper Ralph Boston was the first man on earth to jump over 27 feet.

In 1946, Shaw native Boo Ferris won 13 consecutive games as a pitcher in Fenway Park. It is still a major league record.

Brookhaven's Lance Alworth holds the all-time NFL record for the most 200+ yard receiving games in a career. He accomplished it in five games.

Mississippian Henry Armstrong is the only boxer to ever hold three world titles in different weight classes simultaneously.

Heavyweight champion boxer John L. Sullivan has a couple of Mississippi ties. In 1882, he defeated Paddy Ryan in Mississippi City and was declared World Champ. Another significant Mississippi fight was the last title fight under London Prize Ring Rules — in other words, bare-knuckle fist fighting. Originally scheduled for New Orleans, legal concerns forced the fight to Richburg, Mississippi, south of Hattiesburg. Sullivan defeated Jake Kilrain in round number 75 (back then rounds weren't timed; they lasted until one man hit the deck).

Willye White, a native of Money, was the first American track and field athlete to compete in five Olympics (1956-1972). At the age of 16, she won the silver medal in the long jump at the 1956 Olympics in Melbourne, Australia.

Clarksdale native Charlie Conerly was not just famous as the long-time quarterback of the New York Giants. He was also the first Marlboro Man.

———

Starkville's Cool Papa Bell maintained a .419 batting average during a 28-year career in the Negro Baseball League.

———

McCool native Margaret Wade coached the Delta State Women's Basketball team to three consecutive national titles (including a 51-game win streak). The NCAA Woman Player of the Year trophy bears her name.

———

At the age of 18, Brandon native Devin Britton was the youngest person to ever win the NCAA Men's Singles Tennis Title—he broke John McEnroe's record.

———

Oakland native S.B. Sam Vick was the first and only baseball player to pinch hit for Babe Ruth.

———

LITERATURE &
JOURNALISM

The first Mississippian to win a Pulitzer Prize was Tennessee Williams. He received the award in 1948 for *A Streetcar Named Desire*. Williams was awarded a second Pulitzer in 1955 for *Cat on a Hot Tin Roof*. Williams won three Tony Awards and three New York Drama Critics' Circle Awards. In 1980, he was awarded the Presidential Medal of Freedom.

William Faulkner also won two Pulitzers. His prizes were awarded in 1955 for *A Fable* and in 1963 for *The Reivers*. Twice Faulkner won the National Book Award. In 1950, he won the Nobel Prize.

Eudora Welty was the third Mississippian to be awarded a Pulitzer Prize. In 1973, Welty won for *The Optimist's Daughter*. In 1980, she was awarded the Presidential Medal of Freedom. A National Book Award followed in 1983. In 1998, Welty became the first living author to have her works published in the prestigious Library of America series.

In 1981, Beth Henley became the fourth Mississippian to win a Pulitzer Prize for her play, *Crimes of the Heart*.

In 1996, Richard Ford was awarded the Pulitzer for his novel, *Independence Day*. The book also won the PEN/Faulkner Award — a first for any novelist.

In 2007, Gulfport native Natasha Trethewey won the Pulitzer prize for her collection, *Native Guard*. In 2012, she was named U.S. Poet Laureate. It was the first time a Mississippian has held the distinguished position.

In 2009, Leland native Douglas A. Blackmon was awarded the Pulitzer for *Slavery by Another Name: The Re-Enslavement of Black Americans from the Civil War to World War II*. Blackmon writes for *The Wall Street Journal*.

Mississippi native Barry Hannah was called "the maddest writer in the USA" by Truman Capote. Hannah's work was awarded The William Faulkner Prize, The PEN/Malamud Award for short fiction, and the Award for Literature from the American Academy and Institute of Arts and Letters.

Kathryn Stockett's *The Help* has sold more than 5 million copies. It has been published in 35 countries. A film version was released in 2011 (directed by Mississippian Tate Taylor).

Tula Native Larry Brown was considered one of the finest modern-day Southern writers. Twice he won the Southern Book Award.

———

At the age of 32, author Willie Morris was appointed Editor-in-Chief of *Harper's Magazine* — the youngest in the magazine's 117-year history.

———

Mississippian Ellen Gilchrist was the 1984 National Book Award for her short story collection, *Victory Over Japan*.

———

Greenville native Shelby Foote spent 20 years writing his masterpiece, *The Civil War: A Narrative*.

———

Walker Percy's 1961 novel, *The Moviegoer*, won the National Book Award.

———

In 1983, Alice Walker's *The Color Purple* won the Pulitzer Prize and the National Book Award.

———

John Grisham currently has 275 million books in print. His books have been translated into 29 languages. Nine of his novels have been turned into films.

———

Thomas Harris, a native of Rich, is best known for his Hannibal Lecter series: *Red Dragon*, *The Silence of the Lambs*, and *Hannibal Rising*. All three novels have been turned into films.

———

Tunica native, Charlaine Harris, is best known for her series, *The Southern Vampire Mysteries*. The series inspired the HBO series *True Blood*.

———

Donna Tartt's first novel, *The Secret History*, has sold millions of copies. It has been translated into 24 languages.

———

Holly Springs native Shepard Smith is the highest-rated anchor on the Fox News Network.

———

Pass Christian native Robin Roberts has won three Emmy Awards for her work in broadcasting.

———

Mississippi newspaper editor and publisher Hazel Brannon Smith was the first woman to ever win a Pulitzer Prize for editorial writing. She won the award in 1964 for editorials against social injustice in Mississippi.

Delta native Larry Speakes was press secretary for President Ronald Reagan.

———

Greenville newspaperman Hodding Carter, Jr. was awarded a Pulitzer Prize for Editorial Writing in 1946.

———

Jackson native Charles Overby was editor of *The Clarion-Ledger* when it won the Pulitzer Prize for Public Service. He is chairman and CEO of The Freedom Forum and CEO of the Newseum in Washington D.C.

———

Oxford resident Samir Husni holds the largest private collection of first edition magazines. He owns over 26,000 copies of premier editions.

———

Mississippi native Turner Catledge served as managing editor of *The New York Times* from 1951-1964. Under his leadership, the newspaper won dozens of Pulitzer Prizes.

———

Newspaper-syndicated columnist and Okolona native William Raspberry earned a Pulitzer Prize for Commentary in 1994.

———

Mississippian James Autry served as an editor and publisher at Meredith Corporation, publisher of *Better Homes & Gardens*.

———

Picayune resident Eliza Jane Poitevant Holbrook (aka Pearl Rivers) was the first woman to own a major metropolitan newspaper — the *New Orleans Picayune* in the mid-19th century.

———

THE CIVIL WAR

Union General William Tecumseh Sherman gained fame for his blazing "March to the Sea" through Georgia. He honed his troops with a similar march in 1864 from Vicksburg, through Jackson on to Meridian, and back. Meridian virtually ceased to exist. Brandon, Hillsboro, Morton, Lake, and Marion also suffered severe damage in the raid.

———

Union General William T. Sherman said he feared only two men in the Confederate Army: Gen. Nathan B. Forrest and Jackson resident Gen. Wirt Adams. Adams, like Forrest, was a cavalry commander and was in the thick of almost all fighting in West Tennessee, North Alabama, and North and Central Mississippi from beginning to end. Unscathed from the war, Adams ironically met his doom in an 1888 street duel in the state capital in which he also killed his opponent, a Jackson newspaper editor.

———

Mississippi soil is home to four National Cemeteries in Corinth, Vicksburg, Natchez, and Biloxi.

———

The Corinth National Cemetery was established in 1866. Six thousand Union soldiers are interred in its area and a few Confederates. Most confederate soldiers are buried in mass graves around the perimeter of where the battle was fought in October 1862.

———

Most know Beauvoir was the Confederate States of America President Jefferson Davis's last home, but he owned others. His boyhood home was "Rosemont" in Woodville. And his older brother, Joseph, gave him a large tract of unimproved land full of sticker bushes between Vicksburg and Port Gibson. Davis created a plantation and named it "Brierfield." The shifting Mississippi River cut the farm off from the land. It then became known as Davis Island. In 1897, the river eroded away the island and all of the Davis's land disappeared into the river.

———

One of Mississippi's most prominent Civil War general to be killed in action was William Barksdale. He led troops to victory in a number of engagements in Virginia. He was killed in the Battle of Gettysburg and is buried in Jackson.

———

Mississippi's Civil War estimates for those killed in action or killed later from wounds sustained in action are 8,500. The Civil War estimate for Mississippian soldiers dying from disease is 6,800. The total dead came to 15,300 out of an enlisted 71,000 (22%).

The Tupelo National Battlefield Park is the smallest in the U.S., at one acre.

———

Vicksburg once boasted a castle. The large private residence, built circa 1850, had four towers and a moat. During the Civil War, the castle was owned by a staunch Unionist. Ironically the home was destroyed by Union troops to clear their field of fire for their cannons. The troops called their setup Castle Battery.

———

July 4, 1863 was the day of Vicksburg's surrender. After the fall, the Union command went to work protecting their prize. They feared a future Confederate resurgence like their own recent siege. Gen. Grant ordered all of the dug-out advances and ditches his army had constructed to be filled in and he had new shorter line trenches dug so that fewer soldiers could man the defenses. Vicksburgers did not celebrate the Fourth of July again until 1945.

———

Vicksburg National Cemetery has approximately 17,000 Civil War graves. Of that number, only 4,000 have names; the other 13,000 are unknown soldiers. Three Confederates are among the 17,000.

———

The commander of the losing Confederate force at the Battle of Corinth, Earl Van Dorn, was from Port Gibson. He died during the Civil War, but not in battle. Just a few days after cooler heads talked him out of dueling Nathan B. Forest, Van Dorn left this world by a bullet to the brain from a jealous husband who believed Van Dorn had seduced his wife. Van Dorn's mother, incidentally, was Andrew Jackson's niece.

———

A consensus of historians has noted Mississippi as the scene of 15 Civil War engagements worthy to be listed as battles. They were: Big Black River, Brice's Crossroads, Champion's Hill, Chickasaw Bayou, Corinth, Grand Gulf, Iuka, Jackson, Meridian, Okolona, Port Gibson, Raymond, Snyder's Bluff, Tupelo, and Vicksburg.

———

Gen. Nathan Bedford Forrest is renowned as a great military strategist and was studied by George S. Patton, Norman Schwarzkopf, and Erwin Rommel. Forrest was a warrior general, leading from the front where the danger lied. It is said he had 30 horses shot from under him, was wounded four times, and killed 24 men in hand-to-hand combat during the war. His great grandson was killed over Germany during World War II.

One of the worst (or greatest) cavalry events of the Civil War was Grierson's Raid. In the spring of 1863 Union Col. Benjamin Grierson used his mounted troops to prevent a marshalling of Rebel forces to oppose Gen. Grant's amphibious landing at Bruinsburg. Grierson's 1,700 men began capturing stores and ammunition, freeing prisoners, and destroying railroad stock in New Albany, Pontotoc, Houston, Louisville, Philadelphia, Decatur, Newton, Raleigh, Hazlehurst, Union Church, Brookhaven, and Summit.

———

At the outbreak of the Civil War many students and faculty at the University of Mississippi quit and enlisted. Many formed into Company A, 11th Miss. Infantry or the University Greys. Their most famous incident of the war was Pickett's Charge at Gettysburg. All were killed or wounded.

———

Although fought inside our state's borders, the Battle of Champion's Hill listed only one dead Confederate from Mississippi.

———

Civil War Battles often had more than one name. Champion's Hill was also called the Battle of Baker's Creek. Why? Northern record-keepers named battles after nearby rivers or streams, while the Southerners named them after the closest town. The Battle of Tupelo is also called the Battle of Harrisburg. Brice's Crossroads is also known as the Battle of Tishomingo Creek.

———

North and west of West Point is tiny Big Springs. It is said the local citizenry got into a fight with four Union soldiers during the Civil War, shot them, and secretly buried the bodies outside of town.

———

The Civil War really did pit brother against brother. Natchez resident Charles Dalhgren was a brigadier general in the C.S.A., while older brother, John, was a rear admiral in the Union Navy. John invented the Dalhgren gun (a bottle-shaped, cast-iron cannon). Charles had once lived in the magnificent Natchez mansion "Dunleith."

———

Holly Springs was the site of a significant Confederate coup in 1862 when General Van Dorn raided the town and destroyed all of U.S. Grant's Union Army supplies, forestalling his attack on Vicksburg. Grant's wife and children were in Holly Springs during the raid and Van Dorn sent guards to protect them. In returning a favor, Grant refused to burn Van Dorn's hometown of Port Gibson when marching through in 1863.

During the Civil War, the capital city had an ammunition factory. It was known as the Jackson Arsenal and it manufactured rifle cartridges. In November 1862 forty-nine lives were lost in a huge explosion, most of which were teenage boys and girls. The newspaper description said bodies were hurled 150 yards from the site of the explosion and absolutely nothing was left of the entire two-story brick building.

The first official landowner of what would become Yazoo City was Greenwood Leflore. In 1828 he sold his land, and the new owners named it Manchester. In 1841, to honor the river that supported the community, the residents voted to change the name.

In the Civil War the Confederates established a Navy Yard in 1862 on a nearby channel of the Yazoo River. It was there that the ironclad "Arkansas" was finished. The warship had a short life — three weeks.

In 1862 the Federal warship "Massachusetts" fired cannons on Pass Christian. Confederate troops had been in town, but had moved to Biloxi. One brave woman leaned out of the second story window of her home and began flapping a large white cloth of linen at the ship. It became known as the "Bed Sheet Surrender."

While under Union Army occupation in 1864, the Catholic Bishop of the Natchez Diocese, William Elder, defied the order to lead his congregation in a prayer for Abe Lincoln. Bishop Elder was subsequently arrested, jailed, and banished from Natchez.

For the presidential election of 1860, Abraham Lincoln didn't even appear on the ballot in Mississippi (although Stephen A. Douglas did). Douglas received 4% of the vote. In 1861 when the Southern states seceded, along with South Carolina, Mississippi was the only other state to have a population with whites in the minority.

BUSINESS & COMMERCE

The largest advertising agency in Mississippi is The Godwin Group.

The largest bank in Mississippi (based on assets) is the Tupelo-based Ban-corpSouth. The financial services firm holds more than $13 billion in assets.

The Pearl River Resort is the state's largest casino with more than 200,000 square feet of gaming space.

Horne LLP is the state's largest accounting firm with nearly 100 CPAs.

The largest enrollment in any college in the state is Mississippi State University. Enrollment for 2011 was 15,543.

Keesler Federal Credit Union is the largest in Mississippi with assets of $1.9 billion and more than 180,000 members.

The state's largest employer is Huntington Ingalls Industries. More than 10,800 men and women are employed at the Pascagoula facility.

The largest hospital in Mississippi has 2,109 beds. The official name of the facility is the Mississippi State Hospital. It is better known by its location — Whitfield.

The largest law firm in Mississippi is Butler, Snow, O'Mara, Stevens and Cannada, PLLC. The firm employs 115 attorneys.

Jackson-based Ergon, Inc. is the largest privately-held company in Mississippi. The petroleum refiner and electronics firm has annual sales exceeding $3.6 billion.

Louisville-based Taylor Machine Works started as a small machine shop 80 years ago. Today the company manufactures more than 100 models of industrial lift equipment, including one of the world's largest forklifts, capable of lifting 120,000 pounds.

Oxford-based FNC, Inc. revolutionized the U.S. housing market by pioneering automated valuation. They invented a software system called Collateral Management System that is used by the top mortgage lenders in the U.S.

Ridgeland-based C Spire is the largest privately-held wireless communication firm in the United States.

—————

Meridian's Peavey Electronics is one of the world's largest manufacturers of audio equipment. The company holds 130 patents, as well as 2000+ product designs.

—————

Gulfport's Glenn Mueller, CEO of Domino's franchise RPM Pizza, invented the pizza delivery hot bag, as well as the car-top delivery sign.

—————

Flora-based Primos Hunting produces over 600 separate products and holds 26 patents. They fulfill needs for the turkey, deer, predator, elk and waterfowl hunter.

—————

Dr. Emmette F. Izard of Hazelhurst developed the first fibers of rayon — the first real synthetic material.

—————

Bob Pittman of Brookhaven founded MTV.

—————

Joseph Biedenharn of Vicksburg was the first person to bottle Coca-Cola in 1894.

—————

The first bottle of Dr. Tichener's Antiseptic was produced in Liberty, Mississippi.

—————

Borden's condensed milk was first canned in Liberty .

—————

Columbus native David Harrison owns the patent on the soft toilet seat.

—————

The highest paid profession in Mississippi is physicians. In 2011, the average salary was $221,700.

—————

Year after year, Philadelphia-based Yates construction is ranked at the top of *Engineering News Record*'s listing of the top construction companies in America. In fact, they have been ranked #1 in the nation in the entertainment field, #2 in the multi-unit residential arena, #3 in Automobile Plant construction, and #4 in the realm of manufacturing.

—————

Laurel-based Howard Industries is the world's largest manufacturer of distribution transformers.

Greenwood's Viking Range Corporation, founded by Fred Carl, Jr., developed the first commercial range specifically designed, engineered, and certified for home use.

————

Business ventures owned by the Mississippi Band of Choctaw Indians employ more than 5,000 Mississippians.

————

Oxford resident and retired dentist Don Newcomb opened the first McAlister's Deli in 1989 in a converted gas station. There are currently 300 McAlister's Delis in 23 states.

————

Mississippi native Harry A. Cole, Sr. created Pine Sol in the early 1900s.

————

Tupelo-based Journal Inc. publishes the *Northeast Mississippi Daily Journal*, a 35,000 circulation daily newspaper, as well as 20 weekly newspapers. The company is owned by the nonprofit CREATE Foundation.

————

AGRICULTURE

We tend to think our state produces larger percentages of our nation's cotton and soybeans. Actually those crops account for 3% of the national output. Mississippi produces 17% of all aquaculture in the United States. Our state also produces 10% of all chicken broilers.

————

The most valuable crop, per acre, in the state is not cotton nor soybeans. It is the sweet potato. Chickasaw and Calhoun counties account for 80% of Mississippi's entire production. Gerber Baby Foods is a big client. Many scientists claim that the sweet potato is the most nutritious vegetable in the world.

————

Tobacco farming is generally associated with Virginia and North Carolina. Early Mississippi farmers could roll it out, too. In 1798, farmers grew approximately 1.5 million pounds of tobacco in the Natchez district alone.

————

Mississippi's Quail population has dropped by 70% since 1960. There are 22 quail hunting lodges and shooting preserves scattered around our state. Wildlife experts cite the following factors as contributing to the demise of Mississippi's wild quail population: fire ants, coyotes, brush burning, livestock, mono-agriculture (such as grass or pine tree farms), insecticides, reduction of food sources, and urban sprawl.

————

Feral hogs are found in 65 of Mississippi's 82 counties. The first hogs were brought to Mississippi by Hernando De Soto's troops. Mississippi's wild hogs are a mixed breed of domestic pigs gone feral and the European boar which was intentionally introduced for hunting purposes. Wild hogs are prodigious breeders. In any given year, 75% of the feral hog population must be eliminated to control their numbers.

————

Mississippi's production of peanuts grew from 2000 acres in 2003 to 20,000 acres in 2009. Why, you ask, did Mississippi farmers wait so long to capitalize on what Georgia growers had been doing for decades? Like tobacco and sugar, peanuts were under a federal quota system until 2002.

————

According to the experts at Mississippi State University, 68% of Mississippi is forested land.

————

February is Mississippi's wettest month. Seattle has the reputation for rain, but Jackson, on average, gets 19 more inches per year.

The tallest tree in our state is on U.S. Forest Service land in Scott County. It is a 156-foot tall spruce pine. A 152-foot black willow located in Jefferson County takes second place.

———

The highest temperature on record in Mississippi—115 degrees—was recorded in Holly Springs on July 29, 1930. The lowest temperature, -8 degrees, was recorded in Corinth on January 30, 1966.

———

Mississippi is known as the Magnolia State. The species is named for French botanist, Pierre Magnol. The magnolia is an ancient species—20 million year-old fossils have been discovered. They're durable, too. President Andrew Jackson transplanted a magnolia on the White House grounds in honor of his wife. It is still thriving.

———

The boll weevil came to the U.S. through the Brownsville-Mexico border around 1892, devouring young cotton buds as the species spread to the east. By 1907, boll weevils were discovered in southwest Mississippi cotton fields. Within seven years the beetle had infested the entire state. By 1950, boll weevils had developed a resistance to DDT.

———

Fire ants supposedly entered the United States at Mobile's port in 1919. Twenty years later, Jackson, Greene and, George counties had the ants. By 1995, fire ants had infiltrated every county in the state. Fire ants eat boll weevils and are credited with virtually eradicating boll weevil's from Mississippi's cotton fields.

———

There are 38 times more chickens than people in Mississippi.

———

Agriculture is the second most dangerous profession in the United States (behind mining). In Mississippi, tractors are the major culprit in accidents. A study conducted between 1986 and 2003 showed that tractor rollovers accounted for about half of all agriculture-related deaths. In the decade between 1990 and 2000, we lost 146 Mississippians to tractor accidents.

———

WHAT'S IN
A NAME?

One of the great names of all time is Mississippian Hernando DeSoto Money, from Zieglersville in Carroll County. H.D. Money was a Confederate soldier who later served in Congress, as a representative and senator from 1875 to 1911.

———

L. Q. C. Lamar was a prominent man in his day. Lucius Quintus Cincinnatus Lamar is one of only two men to serve as Congressional Representative, U.S. Senator, Presidential Cabinet member and U.S. Supreme Court Justice.

———

Dizzy Dean had a younger brother who was also a teammate. He sported a nickname, too—Daffy. Known for tales, tall and real, Dizzy once, 6 years after retiring, left the broadcast booth and pitched 4 good innings. In that very game, after pulling a muscle running to first on a single, he was quoted to have said that announcing was his game and was glad he didn't pull a throat muscle. Gone since 1974, but not forgotten, Dizzy is buried in Bond, Mississippi.

———

Working in Memphis in the late 1940s, this Mississippi musician not only played and sang in the clubs, but worked at radio station WDIA as a disc jockey. He went by the on-air-name of "Beale Street Blues Boy." We know him as B.B. as in King.

———

Booneville in Prentiss County was named for a relative of Daniel Boone, Reuben H. Boone. He was head of the first white family to settle in what was then Tishomingo County.

———

Yalobusha County's seat, Coffeeville, is not named after the morning cup of joe, but in fact named for John Coffee. Coffee was a close friend of Andrew Jackson and even served as a second in one of Jackson's duels. He served alongside General Jackson in the Creek Indian War of 1813 and at the Battle of New Orleans in January 1815. He was also instrumental in dealing with the Chickasaw, hammering out treaties and land cessions.

———

Pascagoula native Harry "The Hat" Walker played professional baseball for 15 years, mostly with the St. Louis Cardinals. He would later manage the Pirates and Astros. Playing in the era before batting helmets, Walker earned his nickname from his teammates due to his constant rearranging of his hat when batting, readjusting between every pitch.

Jefferson Davis's mother must have had a good sense of humor. His middle name was Finis which in Latin means "The End." When Davis arrived, he already had nine siblings.

———

One of the all-time names in Mississippi sports is Thad "Pie" Vann. After playing football at Ole Miss, he gained fame at the University of Southern Mississippi where he coached only one losing season out of twenty. He is in the College Football Hall of Fame.

———

Leakesville native "Vinegar Bend" Mizell played his last major league baseball game in 1962.

———

In the running for Mississippi's All-Name Team is Jehu Amaziah Orr. A former Confederate Officer, he later became a state legislator and judge. He was the last surviving member of the Confederate Congress, before dying in 1921 in Columbus.

———

North Mississippi's charming Holly Springs was originally called Suavatooky, which in Chickasaw meant "watering place."

———

Meridian's tallest building, The Threefoot Building, has nothing to do with height. The name is derived from the owners of the edifice, the Threefoot brothers.

———

NATIVE
MISSISSIPPIANS

Mississippi Choctaws Indians sent top secret, military messages during World War I and World War II. They spoke their native tongue over the radio with impunity to the enemies' ears.

———

The Choctaw and Chickasaw men of the 1800s had their own variation of the "duel with pistols at ten paces." To settle dispute, both parties would take the field and upon the word, a close friend would shoot them point blank in the heart. It forced restraint when one might be tempted to issue a dueling threat.

———

The majority of our state's indian mounds are in the Tupelo area. These include Bear Creek, Pharr Mounds, Owl Creek and Bynum Mound. Bynum and Pharr are thought to have been built around 100 A.D. Owl and Bear are believed to have been constructed around 1000 A.D.

———

An old French map from 1719 shows our state's general western and southern borders. It also lists Indian tribes with these identifiable spellings: les Nadchez, les Pascaoocooloos, les Bilochy, les Tonicas, les Tchikachas, and les Yazau. Les Tryou are not identifiable, but were located at the traditional home of the Choctaws.

———

Acknowledging that big cats once roamed far and wide in our state, Copiah County's name translates to English as "calling panther." Coahoma County's name translates to "red panther." Another large predator lends its name to Neshoba County, which translates to "grey wolf." On the milder side, Yalobusha translates to "tadpole place."

———

The 95-mile-long Strong River begins in the Bienville National Forest south of Morton and ends at the Pearl River near the Georgetown vicinity. As local lore has it the river's name does not come from the power of its current, but from its bitter taste. Native Americans' descriptions were mistranslated as "strong."

———

Roughly 25% of our state's 82 counties have names derived from the Native Mississippian language or, in the case of Leflore, are actually named for a Native Mississippian. This is somewhat lower than the national percentage. Fifty percent of our states' names originated from a word in a Native American language.

———

Itta Bena is Choctaw for "forest camp."

The end of the Natchez tribe came about when the French retaliated after the Natchez massacred French settlers. After French soldiers came north from New Orleans a large portion of the Natchez fled to north Mississippi and lived with the Chickasaw. Those who stayed were captured, sold into slavery, and shipped to plantations in the Caribbean.

South of McComb, practically on the Louisiana border, lies the small village of Osyka, Mississippi. Interstate 55 travelers may wonder if the little town has some Japanese connection; actually, it is a variation of a Choctaw word that translates to "soaring eagle."

There's a legend in Noxubee County about a silver mine. In the early 1800s, settlers noticed the Choctaws wore ornamental silver jewelry. To hide their cache, the Choctaw sealed the entrance, abandoned it, and planted six dogwood trees to mark it. The mine, called the Lost Dogwood Mine, is supposedly near Macon.

The ancient Chickasaws of northeast Mississippi carry the moniker "Unconquered Tribe" for good reason. Their formidable fighting capabilities were known far and wide. In the 1700s the French sent three expeditions to wipe them out and were defeated each time.

Neither the written nor spoken Choctaw language uses the letter "R," nor does any Choctaw word begin with the letter "D."

The Treaty of Dancing Rabbit in 1830 marked the final land cession of the Choctaws to the U.S. The Choctaw were the first Native American tribe moved west to what became Oklahoma. Between 1831 and 1833, 13,000 of the 19,000 Mississippi Choctaws were relocated west.

According to one of the missionaries who lived among the Choctaws before their removal, their great ball games were the highlight of the year. A usual match was between two towns, and typically a week-long affair that included much more than just the game. Members of the two towns typically bet personal items, including ponies and clothing, on the outcome of the game.

The Choctaws called our Pearl River "talli yaiya." That translates to "moaning rock." Canoeists and kayakers have claimed to hear a moaning sound on the Pearl at certain times.

In 1779, the governor of Virginia, knowing the Mississippi Chickasaw Indians had long been in league with the English, sent a letter to the tribe warning them to remain neutral. The Chickasaw chiefs responded saying they'd gladly meet the Virginians halfway to fight and predicted they'd chop off a lot of heads. Later, the Chickasaw did send warriors to do battle with the Americans in 1780 at Fort Jefferson in Western Kentucky.

Tishomingo County is named for the last full-blooded Chickasaw war chief, John H. Tishomingo, who died on the Trail of Tears. Iuka is named for his son.

Biloxi is derived from the Choctaw word "biluchi." Translated it means "hickory bark."

Our word in English, Tombigbee, was derived from Native Mississippian "itombi ikbe," which translates to "box maker." It likely refers to limestone slabs found on the namesake river, which were used to house the bones of dead ancestors.

Newton County's town of Chunky has nothing to do with square candy bars. Originally a Choctaw village named Chanki Chitto, it was a place where the Native Mississippians came to compete in sports. They played a game called "tchunkee," which involved rolling polished round stones and opponents hurling spears at them to earn points.

East of Brandon is the small Rankin County town of Pelahatchie. Choctaws hunted and trapped along the winding creek of the same name. Pelahatchie translates to "crooked as smoke."

In the mid-1700s, English traders were settling North Mississippi and inter-marrying with the Native Mississippians—so much so that Colbert is a very common Chickasaw surname. Around 1750, One Levi Colbert, through alert preparation, prevented a Choctaw raiding party from attacking. Pleased by his actions, the tribe gave him a war name of Itte Wamba. This meant "bench sitter," for in Choctaw culture, it was an honor not to be seated on the floor. Later, when the county was organized, they took Itawamba as their name.

Issaquena County was formed in 1844; its name was derived from "deer river" in the Choctaw language.

The Native Mississippian words "bogue" and "hatchie" can be found in many river names. Bogue meant slow moving, dark, mud-bottomed stream; hatchie was used for clearer, faster, rockier streams.

Native Mississippian names abound in Carroll County's waters: Puchshinnubie, Potacocowa, Peachahala, Abotcaputa, and Bucksnubby Branch.

The Native Mississippians known as the Natchez Indians, also seen spelled as "Nochi" by early whites, differed from the Choctaw and other tribes. The Natchez did not worship a spirit of a higher power, but rather the sun. Their head chief was called the Great Sun and his feet were never allowed to touch the ground. He was either carried or had woven straw mats placed before each footfall. The tribe had two distinct classes: the commoners, called Stinkards, and the nobility. The two divisions even spoke different dialects of their own language.

Chickasawhay translates to "place where martins dance."

THE RIVER

Today, Windsor Ruins has 23 standing Corinthian columns. They are 45 feet tall.

———

A little west of Fayette is Springfield Plantation. This was the site of Andrew Jackson's marriage to his beloved wife, Rachel. Rachel was divorced, but at the time of this marriage, 1791, the Spanish-Catholic ruled the area. The only legally recognized marriages were performed by local priests, and Catholic law prohibited a divorced woman at that time to remarry.

———

Jim Bowie's brother, Resin, is buried in Port Gibson at St. Joseph Catholic Church cemetery. The church has blue-stained glass windows that, on a sunny day, cast a cool light purple glow around the church.

———

Natchez City Cemetery houses one of the more interesting graves in Mississippi. After a ten year-old girl died of yellow fever in 1871, her mother had a glass window inserted over the head section of the coffin and a pit with steps and iron-door covers next to the grave. The mother would visit her deceased child during thunderstorms, which had frightened her so when alive.

———

At the age of 20, the infamous Natchez Trace outlaw John Murrell was convicted of stealing horses. Tried and convicted, the frontier judge pronounced sentence of jail time and branding. Murrell was tied to a post in front of the judge's bench. A red-hot poker was placed on the thumb of his left hand, branding the letters H. T. permanently into his skin. Witnesses said he didn't make a sound or even flinch as his skin burned.

———

There are claims that the outlaw Murrell once went to Providence Plantation, near Tchula, Mississippi. Legend has it the Murrell gang would often plant a lone pine in the front yard of a house as a signal that it was a safe haven. Lured into Providence Plantation by a lone pine, Murrell mistakenly went in for breakfast and was taken prisoner by the authorities. He served ten years in prison and died shortly after his release in 1844. Possibly to take revenge on him for leading such a horrific life, his body was buried at a 45-degree angle and laid out facing west, instead of the Christian tradition of east. Later, body snatchers took his head. It was said that for years after, Murrell's head was displayed around at county fairs for 10 cents a look.

Even Mark Twain offered an opinion on the Mississippi bad man, John Murrell. Twain called Frank and Jesse James crime retailers; he called Murrell a wholesaler. Back in the 1820s and 30s, one of Murrell's more common schemes was to gain a slave's trust and convince him to run away. Murrell would then "sell" the slave to a distant plantation. Then, with the slave in cahoots, Murrell would convince him to run again (Murrell promised to share the profits). After a few rounds, Murrell would murder the slave and take all the money. Murrell's trademark was to gut the victim, weigh the body with stones, and sink it in water.

———

A one-time member of Murrell's gang of murdering thieves was Alonzo Phelps. Phelps's hideout was in the southern tip of Yazoo County. Due to its isolation, he managed many a successful escape. His primary targets were boatmen returning north on the Natchez Trace. Lawmen in Yazoo placed a $3,000 bounty on his head, the equivalent of $75,000 today. A local citizen bounty hunter followed Phelps to a widow's cabin. Phelps occasionally preyed on the widow for free food. While engrossed in lunch, Phelps was subdued and taken to Yazoo City. He was shot and wounded while trying to escape and later met his demise at the end of a government rope.

———

The Natchez Trace began its life as a game trail, a path trekked out by deer and buffalo walking through the dense woods. Later use by Native Americans widened the track and by the time of early white exploration it was well known. President Thomas Jefferson wished to gain from its use and pushed to call it the "Columbian Highway." By 1809, after the U.S. Army's improvements, it was passable for wagons. Taverns, inns, and trading posts, known in those days as stands, sprang up on the Trace.

———

Natchez is the oldest settled town on the river. King's Tavern is the oldest building in Natchez. Believers in ghosts say that "Madeline," the murdered lover of tavern proprietor Richard King, haunts the upper story. Legend says King's wife murdered her, then bricked up the corpse behind the fireplace.

———

This 100-year-old+ bed and breakfast in Vicksburg, Stained Glass Manor-Oak Hall, claims to have one guest who never checks out. Supposedly a ghost resides in the old home, but the claim is that he, she, or it can only be seen by children under the age of 8.

Operating in the 1790s and early 1800s, Big Harpe and Little Harpe were known as Land Pirates of the Natchez Trace. They robbed travelers and murdered them. A few estimates put the death toll in the 30s. Some who have studied their villainous lives claim that they were America's first serial killers.

———

Sam Mason was also a notorious Trace highwayman. One of Mason's gang, Little Harpe (in partnership with another gang member) murdered Mason in 1804 in order to collect reward money. The two took Mason's head to the authorities in Claiborne County. Previous robbery victims recognized the two and, instead of a reward, they received a trial and death by hanging.

———

Today our word "gulf" denotes a large body of water surrounded by three sides of land. In the nineteenth century, it meant what today we refer to as a whirlpool. Hence the Claiborne County town of Grand Gulf literally translats as "large whirlpool."

———

John James Audubon was sent to America from France by his father to escape conscription into Napoleon's Army. He frequently visited Mississippi to hunt and draw our native animal life. In 1822 he was a teacher at the Elizabeth Female Academy, near Natchez. Audubon made his living in New Orleans drawing portraits of travelers in Jackson Square.

———

Six miles south and east of Port Gibson is the tiny map dot known as Tillman. Here, in the early 1800s, there was a great mansion home called La Cache. It belonged to a wealthy English immigrant, Harman Blennerhasset. Aaron Burr hid at La Cache when being chased by the authorities for complicity in the Southwest Conspiracy (Burr's never-proven plan to shave off Texas and other lands and make a nation independent of the United States). Blennerhasset, at the age of 31, had been shamed from England for marrying his 18-year-old niece.

———

THE COAST

The Alamo Plaza Motor Inn on Highway 90 in Gulfport had a distinctive, stylized Spanish mission façade over its main and two outer buildings. It was set among a grove of gorgeous live oaks. It was demolished in 2003.

———

The Barq's Bottling Company has roots in New Orleans dating back to 1890, but moved to Biloxi and began bottling root beer seven years later. Coca-Cola bought out the local company in 1995.

———

St. Stanislaus College in Bay St. Louis was founded in 1854 by Brothers of the Sacred Heart Order. In 1923 it became a college prep school. It is now a male-only boarding school for grades 7 through 12.

———

Biloxi's Keesler Air Force Base is named for Greenwood, Mississippi native Samuel Reeves Keesler. During World War I as a gunner on a reconnaissance flight over Verdun, France, Keesler battled four German fighters.He lost his life in the ensuing dogfight and was awarded a posthumous Silver Star Medal.

———

The first quarantine station in the country was founded in 1880 on Ship Island.

———

Elmwood Manor, a fine old home in Bay St. Louis, served as training headquarters for the Saenger Amusement Company. In 1924 the company owned and operated theatres in 12 Southern states and had 320 movie houses. Saenger owned, or partly owned, theatres scattered all over, in any Mississippi town of size.

———

At the present site of Buccaneer State Park, near Waveland, stood a grand old home. Legend says that Andrew Jackson lived there, but historians disagree, stating it was Andrew Jackson, Jr. The house burned, twice, and then was finally destroyed by the Hurricane of 1947.

———

The yacht club in Pass Christian, established in 1849, is the second oldest in the United States.

———

The Biloxi City Cemetery is also known as the Old French Cemetery and has been in use for 300 years. In it lies a Medal-of-Honor winner for actions against Cheyenne Indians in 1877; the first African-American Roman Catholic Archbishop; and Jeff Davis's nephew who himself was a Confederate Brigadier General.

During World War II, only one German U-boat sank in the Gulf of Mexico. It sank due south of the Mississippi coast at the mouth of the Mississippi River. U-166 was sunk by depth charges dropped from a Coast Guard PBY airplane. A few days earlier, the U-166 had sunk a passenger steamer named "Robert E. Lee." They both lie on the gulf floor less than one mile apart.

―――

Gulfport owes its creation to two men: William Hardy and Capt. Joseph Jones. Hardy was a lawyer by trade and became president of the Gulf and Ship Island Railroad. He was the idea man who dreamed of a railroad touching the Gulf and leading north into the great Piney Woods lumber source. Captain Jones was a rich Pennsylvania oil man who was intrigued by trains. Shot down by Congress on his idea of dredging a channel from Ship Island to the railroad's lumber pier in tiny Gulfport, Jones paid for it himself.

―――

Jefferson Davis' last home, Beauvoir, was originally built in Biloxi in 1852. The widow of the first owner sold the property in 1873 to Sarah Dorsey. Mrs. Dorsey agreed to sell Beauvoir to Jefferson Davis for $5000, payable in three installments. Davis made one payment and then with Dorsey's death discovered he'd inherited the property. After his death, Beauvoir became an old soldiers' home. Three Confederate widows lived on the property until 1957 when they were removed to a nursing home.

―――

Ship Island's masonry fort was under construction during the Civil War with walls only six feet high when the Union ship "U.S.S. Massachusetts" shelled the Confederates there. The Rebel forces soon left the island and Union troops completed the construction, taking control of the strategic spot. At that time, the fort was located at the island's midpoint. Due to erosion, Fort Massachusetts now sits on the westernmost point.

―――

One of the pre-Great Depression hotels in Mississippi was the Pine Hills-on-the-Bay Hotel located at the north end of the Bay of St. Louis. The erection of an automobile bridge across the bay and the Stock Market Crash of '29 doomed the hotel.

―――

In central Jackson county was once a tiny hamlet named Brewton. Off the commercial path, the community began to shrink and die. Just before passing into history, the remaining residents (or resident) re-named Brewton, Wontierioniasiopolis.

In 1990 the state legislature approved dockside gaming, but gambling had been around long before that. Slot machines and roulette wheels mostly existed in bars and hotels on the Coast. In the 50s and 60s anti-gambling sentiment from churches, businessmen and military brass increased, along with calls for the enforcement of the existing laws which were being ignored. By 1970 the machines were gone.

———

An ex-officer, Col. Lopez of the Spanish Army, gathered 400 men onto Round Island, off the coast of Pascagoula. Most were former U.S. soldiers from the Mexican War. Lopez intended to overthrow the Spanish rulers of Cuba but word leaked and President Zachary Taylor quelled the little uprising by blockading Round Island with 3 U.S. warships. Lopez and 50 followers eventually made it to Havana. A firing squad took care of his men, while Lopez was garroted in the public square. The liberation flag Lopez brought with him ended up being Cuba's official flag after the Spanish-American War, roughly fifty years later.

———

Long Beach's giant Friendship Oak is estimated to have been a seedling at the time of Columbus's first voyage to the New World. Its trunk has a circumference of nearly 20 feet. Ocean Springs boasts a monster live oak, too—the Ruskin Oak. Its trunk measures 21-feet in circumference.

———

The outlaw James Copeland started his career at an early age. At age 12 he was charged with larceny for selling stolen property. He was guilty and his mother knew it, but it wasn't his first crime. Fearing prison for her son, she enlisted help from a friend of a friend and arranged for a shady character named Wages to help. Mr. Wages took James with him one night and burned down the entire Jackson County Courthouse — destroying the records of James' crimes and freeing him from the charges.

———

James Copeland gave Jesse James and Billy the Kid a good run for their place in crime history. Copeland and partners McGrath and Wages amassed $30,000 in gold by 1845 (equal to nearly $1,000,000 today). They buried their gold in the Catahoula Swamp in central Hancock County and made a map. Later, during a gunfight to avenge the deaths of his partners, Copeland lost the map. Copeland went into hiding. The gold was eventually discovered and stolen. The Mobile newspapers carried accounts of the gold being found, but after a few generations, it was a better story for the gold to still be somewhere in the swamp and a tale of lost treasure was born.

The Jackson County based Wages-Copeland Gang of outlaws was, if nothing else, bold. In the 1830s, Mobile, like most towns, had a volunteer fire department. The gang set fires to the portion of Mobile on the west side of the bay. While the east residents came over to battle, or just watch, the fire, the gang looted houses and stores on the eastern side of the bay. A year later, the gang repeated the same ruse, only burning the east and robbing the west.

James Copeland's outlaw career ended with his hanging in 1857. A body snatcher dug up his corpse and cleaned the flesh off. A doctor wired the bones together and made a standing skeleton. The skeleton was displayed in his office until it was later given to a drug store in Hattiesburg. Around 1900 someone broke into the store, and stole Copeland's bones . . . but nothing else.

At one time, there were more barrier islands off the Mississppi coast. Located between Ship and Horn Island, due south of Ocean Springs, was a 400-acre spit of sand called Dog Island. In the days of Prohibition, three Biloxi businessmen invested and built a resort to capitalize on it being outside of the United States International Boundary (and outside U.S. laws). To sound more befitting a luxury beach adult playground, the businessmen changed the island's name to Isle of Caprice. By 1926 a gambling casino, dance hall, restaurant, bar, and bath house existed on the island. Tragically, visitors made a habit of picking sea oats to take home for decoration. As the barrier islands are prone to do in the presence of erosion, storm winds, and shifting sea currents, the isle began to sink—by 1932 it was totally submerged.

Again in the mid 1980s, to circumvent the no gambling laws, Biloxi Harbor moored a 150-foot ship that was expressly fitted out for gambling. It was named the "Europa Star" with specialties of "cruises to nowhere" out beyond the international boundary.

Picayune can attribute its name to a female New Orleans newspaper owner. Her real name was Eliza Jane Poitevant Holbrook (though she wrote under the pseudonym Pearl Rivers). At the turn of the last century, the railroad was coming through the small Mississippi community of Hobolochitto and the citizens asked Mrs. Nicholson to help change their name. She really liked the name of her newspaper, The Times Picayune, and thus it was shared with the locals.

The eighty-mile-long Pascagoula River holds the distinction of being the last free-flowing river in the continental United States. The river is better known locally as "The Singing River." The river makes a noise somewhat like a stir of swarming bees in the summer and fall.

The Mississippi coast population grew 17% in the 1990s. During the same period, coast tourist visitation went from 1.5 million to 11.5 per year. The reason: casinos.

How did Pass Christian get its unusual name? Early French explorers had called the water between the mainland and Cat Island "Oyster Pass." Later settlers borrowed the name of a second-generation Cat Island resident by the name of Nicholas Christian Ladner and the water pass. The land mass took on the combination of his middle name and the original French, becoming Pass Christian.

Today's Interstate 10 stretches from Los Angeles to Jacksonville, FL. Constructions on its precursor started in 1915, running from St. Augustine FL. to San Diego and was called the Old Spanish Trail. We now know it as U.S. Highway 90 on the coast.

Our first official state highway map dates from 1928. The map legend listed four types of roads: paved or improved surface, gravel, graded dirt and unimproved dirt. At that time there were approximately 325 miles of paved road in the entire state.

A Biloxi resident owned the state's first automobile in 1900. He also had the first automobile wreck (three days after he purchased the car). Shortly after, Biloxi imposed the first speed limit in the state: 8 miles per hour.

The Mississippi Coast once had its own conclave of former Apollo astronauts. Apollo 13 veteran, Fred Haise, is a Biloxi native. Colorado transplant and Apollo 14 pilot, Stuart Roosa, moved to Gulfport in the early 1980s.

Five years before statehood, Jackson County was created when Mobile County was reduced. Industry has long been the mantra for Jackson County. Records of commercial shipbuilding trace as far back as the 1830s, a tradition that continues today at the state's largest private employer, Ingalls Shipbuilding.

In the early 1700s French explorers in our gulf waters named Cat Island. Unfamiliar with the island's raccoon population, the explorers believed, from a distance, that the racoons were feline. Fittingly, the northernmost spit of land on the island is called Raccoon Swash.

———

SOUTH MISSISSIPPI

In south Mississippi, "Dummy Line Road" signs are common. During the lumber boom, railroads laid track into the vast woods to speed up the lumber loading process. These rail lines, never intended for passengers or any populated destinations, were called dummy lines.

———

The Morgantown community can claim Red Bluff, a cluster of highly eroded hills many call "The Grand Canyon of Mississippi."

———

Greene County is home to Skull Creek Hill and Gnats Bluff.

———

Port Gibson's military prep school, Chamberlain-Hunt Academy, was mentioned in the 1964 Warren Report because Lee Harvey Oswald had two older brothers who'd been cadets there in the late 1940s.

———

A new lake created in 2007 is our state's deepest at 80 feet. It is in our southwest section, in the Meadville and Bude area and is called Lake Okhissa. Pro fisherman and TV host, Bill Dance, helped plan its creation and structure.

———

Go to Stone County and see the world: Texas, India and Wiggins.

———

Before the car, travelers needed to know where to stop. Many old state maps from the 1800s show a place simply marked "Water Holes." The spot is just north of the Louisiana state line, on the county lines of Pike and Marion.

———

If strangers passed through southern Smith County and wound up in Sullivan's Hollow there was a good chance they might be shot, stabbed, hitched to a mule and forced to plow, whipped, hanged, or even all of the above. The town of Mize is Sullivan's Hollow capital. Nine Sullivan brothers from South Carolina settled the area in about 1810. One brother gained the nickname "Hog," so given by other settlers based on the disappearance of their pigs. The Sullivans had trouble amongst themselves. A running fifty-year feud, complete with murders, lasted until 1910.

———

Captain William H. Hardy was a pioneer lumberman and civil engineer. He founded Hattiesburg, the "Hub City," in 1882 and presented it as a gift to his wife. It was Hattie's burg and named in her honor.

———

Perry County claims Shut Eye Creek and Hercules Station.

A few of George County's locales include Boneyard Lake, Booger Hole Slough, and Mouthful.

———

Just off Highway 49 in Stone County is the town of Wiggins. Like most towns in the state it is named after an original early homesteader. It is unique in that Wiggins was the first name of settler — Wiggins Hatten.

———

Today, our six coast counties make up what used to be Spanish West Florida. The U.S. believed they'd bought them in the 1803 Louisiana Purchase. Spain disagreed. In 1810 the Anglo-American settlers there revolted and for 90 days were a republic, until absorbed by the U.S. While a republic, they made a flag, known as the Bonnie Blue Flag.

———

Simpson County's tiny town of D'Lo proportionally sent more men off to fight in World War II than any other town in the United States.

———

Lawrence County was named for War of 1812 naval hero James Lawrence. Lawrence died in battle with a British warship. Before his passing he told his men, "Don't Give up the Ship." It became the U.S. Navy rallying cry.

———

Franklin County has Goober Creek and Veto.

———

U.S.M. was originally named Mississippi Normal College.

———

Perry, Lawrence, and Jones County are all landlocked counties named after U.S. Naval heroes. Perry is named for Commodore Oliver Hazard Perry, hero of War of 1812 battles on Lakes Erie and Champlain. Perry's flagship at the Battle of Lake Erie was "U.S.S. Lawrence," named for his friend killed earlier in the war. Jones is for John Paul Jones who earned his salt in the Revolution.

———

In 1895, Gulfport had a population of 79 people, no railroad or express office, but did have a post office.

———

Camp Shelby, south of Hattiesburg, is the largest state-owned training site in the nation. The camp was established in 1917 and serves as the destination for over 100,000 Reservists and Guardsmen each year. The camp is the largest National Guard training center east of the Mississippi River.

There was a small naval engagement offshore of Bay St. Louis in the War of 1812. Using Ship Island as their base, British forces manned a fleet of barges and paddled their way toward Louisiana and their attack on New Orleans. A fleet of American gunboats challenged the barges. The American leader was Thomas Catesby Jones, who was wounded in battle and captured. Later in his career Jones returned a deserter named Herman Melville to America and told him the tale of a whale once attacking one of his ships.

———

Forrest County has Upper Dead River and Pistol Ridge.

———

Gulf Park College in Long Beach operated for 50 years. It was an all-girls school and was recognized as one of the leading junior colleges in the South.

———

George W. Bush became the first sitting President to speak at a community college graduation. In 2006 he presided over ceremonies at Mississippi Gulf Coast Community College.

———

The town on the southwest border of our state is Pickneyville. Resting in the grave there is Oliver Pollock, famous for inventing the dollar sign in 1778.

———

Before it closed in 1964, Jefferson Military College, outside of Natchez, was the second oldest chartered military school in the country.

———

In Lauderdale County you'll find Whynot, Complete and Zero.

———

New Augusta in Perry County is two miles south of Old Augusta (it moved in 1906 after realizing what happens to towns not located on the railroad). Lawrence County has New Hebron which moved from Hebron for the same reason.

———

Fort Massachusetts on Ship Island was listed as an active defense fort by the U.S. Military until 1903.

———

In the early 1800s, a Pass Christian resident known as Captain Dave supposedly buried $20,000 in gold coin in a grove of oaks on his property and left—never returning to claim the money.

The waters of Harrison County include Mud Hole and Tail of the Square Handkerchief Shoal. There's also a community named Community.

———

In Lamar County one can find these waters: Tick Creek and Deserters Island.

———

In Jackson County you have Smear Bayou and Lake Catch-em-All.

———

There is a Little Red Schoolhouse in Amite County. In its heyday it was a girls' college known as the Amite Female Academy. When the Union troops came to burn it in 1863, the college's president and the Union commander recognized each other as old friends and the building was spared the torch, but not the eleven pianos, which were taken out and burned.

———

Hancock County can be proud of Rotten Bayou and Napoleon.

———

Wilkinson County has a town named Pond.

———

In 1840 Amite County attempted to leave the State of Mississippi and join Louisiana over arguments about Oxford being chosen as the site for the state university.

———

Some streams of Claiborne County are Hardtimes Branch, Whisky Branch, and Cool Boiler Bayou

———

Jefferson County has Spithead Towhead stream, Baptizing Slough, and the town of Red Lick.

———

Marion County has the town of Improve.

———

Columbia was originally called Lott's Bluff. In 1819 its name was changed to Columbia and is our state's fourth oldest town. Columbia was the last stop in life for one Sylvester Magee. During the 1960s, Sylvester's claim to fame was that he was the last living slave in the United States, having been born into slavery in Enterprise in 1841. When he died, if his claims were true, he would have been 130 years old.

———

CENTRAL MISSISSIPPI

In downtown Jackson, State Street intersects (from south to north) with the streets Tombigee, Pascagoula, Pearl, Amite, Yazoo, and Mississippi. The streets are named after Mississippi rivers—in order from east to west.

———

In the early 1820s Hinds County was tremendous, composed of today's Rankin, Madison, Simpson, Copiah, Yazoo, Bolivar, Sunflower, Holmes, Sharkey, Humphreys, Issaquena, and, of course, Hinds.

———

The Ross Barnett Reservoir, adjoining the junction of Hinds, Rankin and Madison Counties, had problems in the mid 1980s. Someone introduced goats on the small islands dotting the eastern end of the lake and they multiplied out of control.

———

In 1962, while Ross Barnett Reservoir was under construction, workmen discovered the bones of a 40-million-year-old, prehistoric whale. Ross Barnett Reservoir was initially called the Pearl River Reservoir.

———

During World War II the airport in Jackson, Hawkins Field, took on the name of Jackson Army Airbase. The Nazi conquest of The Netherlands forced their government into exile and Hawkins Field became the new home base of their air force and training of their pilots.

———

Mississippi was the first state to ratify the 18th Amendment (Prohibition). In 1966 Mississippi was still "dry" — not having ratified the 21st Amendment to repeal Prohibition. An incident one night probably provided a little more than a slight nudge to get the legislators' attention. Paul Johnson, Jr. was governor and understood the irony of the state collecting taxes on illegal alcohol production. That year's Jr. League Mardi Gras Ball at the Jackson County Club was raided and law enforcement absconded and destroyed the booze. The party was well-attended by prominent businessmen and state politicians. Soon after that, we became the last state ratify the amendment.

———

The Casey Jones Museum is in the town of Vaughn. Jones was a famous railroad engineer in the heyday of train travel. It was in April 1900 that his train left Memphis for Canton an hour and half late. Records show that he'd made up the lost time, but tragedy struck. At the station in Vaughn, four cars of a southbound freight had been left on the track. Casey stayed aboard to attempt a stop. The crash killed him, but no one else on either train.

In 1900, Steen's Creek was a small village due south of Jackson in Rankin County. With a boom in cotton and lumber, a railroad was to be built connecting Gulfport to Jackson. Not wanting to miss out on the commerce, the powers-that-be in Steen's Creek donated land to the railroad for a depot. To sweeten the pot, they even changed the town's name to Florence, the wife of the railroad owner.

In 2004 the Amtrak "City of New Orleans" derailed outside of Flora. The entire train — engine, baggage car, and eight passenger cars — came off the track. The cause was blamed on track shifting. Of the 61 passengers, one lost his life.

At the top of our state Capital is an eagle that is 8 feet tall and has a 15-foot wingspan. The big bird shines brightly from the gilded gold plate covering its solid copper composition. The Illinois Central Railroad actually paid for the building's construction cost, as they owed back taxes. Today's legislators still use the original desks from the "new" Capitol's 1903 opening.

The 2012 Mississippi State Fair, held annually in Jackson, will be the 153rd. The 2011 fair boasted almost 700,000 attendees. Maps of Jackson from the 1830s show that the fair still takes place on the same grounds the first city planners intended.

Our state's third governor, Walter Leake, was also our first U.S. Senator. Leake was a Virginian by birth and a Revolutionary War veteran. He died in 1825 in Mt. Salus, which later became Clinton.

Just east of Byram is the swinging bridge, a wire suspension bridge built in 1905. The bridge is still used today, though only for pedestrian traffic.

Near downtown Jackson, the Boyd House, called "The Oaks," and the Manship House are two of the very few buildings to have survived the Civil War. "The Oaks" was built in 1853. The Manship House in 1857.

Jackson's Clarion Ledger is easily the largest newspaper in the state and traces it roots back to 1837. It ranks as the second oldest in the state, after The Woodville Republican—founded in 1823.

Webster County towns include Fame and Mantee.

There is a volcano under the entire city of Jackson. It has been dormant for 65 million years.

———

The locals know, but for travelers of I-55 north of Jackson at Ridgeland, that miniature replica of the Washington Monument was not built expressly to honor our first president. It hides a cell phone tower.

———

Jackson's Old Capitol went out of daily use in 1903 and sat vacant until 1917. At that time, the building began serving as offices for state employees until 1959. Then Gov. J. P. Coleman spearheaded efforts to transform it into the great museum it is today.

———

On State Street in Jackson is Millsaps College, named for founder Major Rueben W. Millsaps. He was a successful cotton broker and banker and donated the money necessary to open the Methodist school. Their sports teams are known as the Majors.

———

The great architect, Frank Lloyd Wright, was credited as the designer of four Mississippi homes. Three were coastal homes destroyed by hurricanes. The sole survivor is "Fountainhead" in Jackson, also known as the J. Willie Hughes House.

———

Attala County's seat, Kosciusko, did not always go by the name of the great Polish patriot. It was originally known as Red Bud Springs, then Peking, then Paris. One of the local politicians was a relative of General Kosciusko.

———

Warren County towns include Rawhide and Bovina.

———

Castalian Springs, north of Durant, was once a thriving spa between 1870 and 1925. Those were the heydays of healing water spas in Mississippi, such as Owens' Wells, Allison's Wells, Ramsey Springs, and Stafford Springs.

———

Carroll County's website proudly boasts that the whole county is rural: no shopping centers, hospitals, radio or TV stations, and not a single stoplight. They do, however, have a dentist, a pharmacy, a weekly newspaper, and three doctors.

———

Newton County's towns include Volcan and Bissaasha.

Clarke County can claim Greasy Creek.

In Meridian, the airport is named Key Field. The name was derived from a pair of brothers who ran a flying school there. In 1935, to attract attention to the financially struggling airport, the brothers set the World Record for continuous flight—27 consecutive days aloft. That record has never been equaled.

Jones County can claim Noggin Head Branch. It also houses the town of Service.

Houston, in Chickasaw County, was named for Texas hero Gen. Sam Houston who was a personal friend of the land speculator selling lots for the new settlement in 1837.

Col. Louis Winston, prominent lawyer, judge, and colonel of the militia, inspired both Winston County and its county seat, Louisville.

In Kemper County you'll find the town of Wahalak, which means "running water" in Choctaw.

In Winston County, near Louisville, there once was a great pine tree. It was grand enough, in fact, to garner the name "Old Boss." Standing 120 feet high, Old Boss" was hit by lightning in 1920. When the tree was harvested, the stump was 7 feet in diameter the first limb was found to have been 91 feet above the forest floor.

Humphreys County waterways: Silent Shade Cut-Off and Deadman Lake.

Issaquena County has a town named Poverty Point. The county has no public schools.

With no banks around, T.P. Gore supposedly buried his $400,000 fortune in the grounds of his plantation, which later grew into the community of Gore Springs.

The Ross Barnett Reservoir, near Jackson, is relatively shallow. The average depth is about twelve feet. However, the old pre-dam channel of the Pearl River has depths up to fifty feet.

South of Morton, in Scott County, there is still a hamlet of Stage; the little town was originally on the stagecoach route. Later when the trains replaced the horse, Stage changed its name to Track. Still later, around the turn of the last century the name reverted back to Stage.

———

The Nissan Plant in Canton churns out approximately 400,000 autos a year. The facility is 3.5 million square feet. 4,000 people work at the Canton plant. On average, it takes a bit more than 28 hours from the time workers start on a new car until another worker drives a finished one off the line.

———

Towns in Jefferson Davis County include Hooker Hollow and Society Hill.

———

Holmes County can claim Albino Landing.

———

Sharkey County has Devil's Elbow Bayou, as well as the town of Africa.

———

Leflore County towns include Mayday and Money.

———

Kemper County, where De Kalb is located, is named for Rueben Kemper. In the early 1800s, Kemper had some land claims outside Baton Rouge, which the ruling Spanish did not recognize, so they deported Kemper. Kemper returned to the Mississippi territory and raised a small army to march on Baton Rouge and with Anglo-American help hoped to overthrow the Spanish. The settlers did not revolt and Kemper fled back to Mississippi and was arrested.

———

Attala County has these locales: Nile and Mississippi No Name Dam # 5.

———

Jasper County has the community of Success.

———

Columbus Air Force Base was initially called Kaye Field, named after Sam Kaye, a Columbus native, World War I flying ace, and close friend of Eddie Rickenbacker. However the name had to be changed as pilots had trouble discerning Kaye or Key Field (which was in nearby Meridian) when heard over radio.

The Pearl River got its name from early Frenchmen exploring the river's mouth who found oysters and the occasional pearl therein.

———

About ten miles south of Forest and east of Stage is a tiny blip of a place surrounded by dense pines. It's rather old, by our standards, having been settled in the 1830s, and was a stop on the stagecoach line to Brandon. The town was originally called Hell's Half Acre, then Buck Snort, and finally, as it is still known today, Homewood.

———

Fifty miles north of Jackson, in Holmes County, travelers see the exit sign for The Little Red Schoolhouse. A two-story red brick building with a cornerstone laid in 1847 remains at the site. It was actually Eureka Masonic College and birthplace to the organization called Order of the Eastern Star. The last session of schooling was in 1959.

———

In Simpson County there is a locale called Merry Hell. Legend has it the name came about from the Sullivan Clan gatherings where the men drank and transformed into merry hellions.

———

Mississippi once had a train tunnel. It was built around the time of the Civil War, at Lost Gap, just west of Meridian—maintenance was expensive so the tunnel was dynamited in the 1960s.

———

Yazoo County towns: Scotland and Liverpool.

———

The long ago residents of Hillsboro, in Scott County, did not take losing lightly. When Forest was named the county seat in 1866, a courthouse was needed and construction began. Under the cover of night, Hillsboro residents tore up the foundation, then burned the frame, and later began stealing the bricks in efforts to prevent its completion. The people of Forest began armed campouts on the site to protect the courthouse project.

———

Our state governor's mansion was built in 1842 and holds tenure as the second longest continuously occupied governor's mansion in the USA. The architect was William Nichols, who also designed the Lyceum and Old Capitol.

———

Winston County has a town called Deposit.

Before our state capital was named Jackson, it was called LeFleur's Bluff. Before Lefleur's Bluff, the area was known as Parkerville. There was a Choctaw Indian settlement in the same location before that named Chisa Foka. And there was always the unofficial nickname after the Civil War of Chimneyville.

NORTH
MISSISSIPPI

A terrible train accident occurred three miles south of Oxford in February, 1870. A passenger train lost a wheel. It tore up the track on a 50-foot-high trestle, causing the trailing cars to derail. Twenty people died immediately. Forty later died from injuries.

———

Pontotoc County towns include Possom Trot and Toccopola.

———

The small town of Coldwater in Tate County dates back to 1856, founded as Elm Grove. When the Arkabutla Dam and Lake were built in the early 1940s, Coldwater would have become Underwater, so the entire town moved to a new location a mile and half south.

———

Surrounded by treeless, flat farmland, Mississippi's Parchman is a prison without a main exterior wall.

———

In 1801 the Natchez Trace was deemed a federal road and regular mail service between Nashville and Natchez began. The riders met halfway to swap bags and get fresh horses in the town of Tockshish (in Pontotoc County). Tockshish is a Chickasaw word for "tree root." Mail took 12 days to make the entire one-way trip.

———

Prentiss Coounty burgs: Hobo Station, Cairo, Altitude. Streams include Hornolucka Creek and Pee Dee Creek.

———

The early white settlers to Oktibbeha County were drawn to an area of two large springs. A sawmill was erected and began making clapboards for construction. A settlement popped up and was called Boardtown. In 1835, the townspeople voted to change the name in honor of Revolutionary War hero, General John Stark.

———

Coahoma County waterways include Montezuma Bend, Melancholy Bayou, and Moon Lake.

———

Quitman County has communities named Oliverfried and Darling.

———

The Tupelo Automobile Museum features more than 100 classic cars including a rare Tucker. Recently, a 1948 Tucker brought nearly three million dollars at an auction.

———

Grenada County gives us Futheyville and Butputter Creek.

Delta State University in Cleveland is the only school in the state to offer a degree in Commercial Aviation. The school owns and operates 21 aircrafts. Delta State's official mascot nickname is the "Statesmen," which came about in tribute to State Senator Walter Sillers' diligent efforts to have a university placed in Cleveland. The Fighting Okra came about in the mid 80s as students tried to garner support for a fiercer-sounding mascot.

The "W" in Columbus was originally known as Industrial Institute and College. It took a Supreme Court ruling in the early 1980s to break the women-only admissions policy. The latest stats showed an 85-15 female-to-male ratio there.

Ole Miss is known for its Hotty Toddy chant at football games. But what is a hot toddy? The traditional Southern recipe is bourbon, hot tea, honey and a lemon slice or cinnamon stick, served warm, by damn.

South of Oxford is the tiny community of Paris. It's an old place, having been settled in 1836 by doctor and local store owner, Dr. William L. Parris. The town took his name, but left out an '"R."

In Tallahatchie County you'll find Needmore, Brazil, and Wrong Prong.

Tippah County towns include Anvil and Muddy. It also has Bumpass Creek.

The oldest Mississippian ever recorded was Bettie Wilson from New Albany. She was born in 1890 and died in 2006. At the time of her passing, at 115 1/2 years old, she had 38 great-great-great grandchildren.

Up in DeSoto County you'll find the communities of Bullfrog Corners, Love, and Walls.

Lafayette County's Toby Tubby Creek was named for a real person — a Chickasaw chief who ran a ferry on the Memphis-Oxford stage coach line.

Authorities studying the official records and maps of the DeSoto expedition place the Spanish Conquistadors' first sighting of the Mississippi in Tunica County at Commerce Landing, near old Willow Point.

Tunica County settlements include Pink and Clack. County waters include Dead Man Lake and Reel Lake.

In 1932, the infamous Machine Gun Kelly robbed the Citizen's Bank in Tupelo—his last bank robbery. Some in the northern press mistakenly named Pretty Boy Floyd as the perpetrator. Incensed, Floyd wrote a letter to a Tupelo newspaper denying his involvement. Back in 1917, Machine Gun Kelly had briefly been a student at Mississippi State.

Union County communities include Plentitude and Pumpkin Center.

Corinth's specialty, the Slugburger, is not made from the mollusc. The name probably came from the burger's cost of a nickel or, as some call it, a slug. The traditional recipe is ground beef mixed with soybean grits served on a burger bun with pickles, mustard, and onions.

Lick Skillet Creek runs through Itawamba County.

Washington County waters include Hoots Dump Slough and Puzzle Bayou. It also has a community called Bourbon.

Columbus is home to our oldest public school, Franklin Academy. It was founded in 1821.

Some Lee County towns include Jug Fork and Frog Island.

In Corinth is a unique little store that makes uniforms and other accoutrements to outfit Civil War re-enactors (as well as uniforms for earlier U.S. wars). Most everything is handmade. They serve both north and south.

Bolivar County streams bear the most descriptive names: Dry Bayou, Straight Bayou, Stillwater Bayou, Icy Bayou, and Thousand Yard Bayou.

The Tri Lakes of the Hills are Sardis Lake, Lake Enid, and Grenada Lake. Sardis is the oldest (completed 1940). Enid's construction ended in 1952. Grenada is the largest lake in the state and newest of the Tri Lakes (finished 1954). The World Record Big Head Carp was landed at Sardis. Enid claims the World record White Crappie at 5lb, 3 oz. Grenada holds two state records: Longnose Gar and White Bass.

Of all our counties, Calhoun County has to have the smallest town to serve as its county seat—Pittsboro has a population of less than 240. It is, however, located at the geographic center of Calhoun County. It is said that Pittsboro was a compromise, both Calhoun City and Bruce both wanted the designation of county seat.

———

In 1960 there were over 70 drive-in movie locations open in Mississippi. As of today, none remain in business. Guntown, Iuka, and Pontotoc had representatives of the last few to survive into the 2000s.

———

Northern Mississippi's town of Ripley has one of the longer-standing commercial activities in the state. Each month on the weekend before the first Monday, they hold a giant flea market at their fairgrounds. Ripley's "First Monday" sale has been happening since 1893...believe it or not.

———

Monroe County isn't encouraging swimmers. In it you'll find Poison Pond & Slunge Creek.

———

Tishomingo County towns include Bugg Landing and Mad Dog Branch.

———

Here's one way to measure Elvis's success: boyhood home in Tupelo, 450 square feet; Graceland Mansion, 17,553 square feet.

———

MISCELLANY &
MINUTIA

During a three-month period when Mississippi was a sovereign state (after it seceded from the Union, but before joining the Confederacy), government officials decreed that a flag be created. The result was "The Magnolia Flag." The flag had a solid white field with a lone magnolia tree in its center and a blue canton surrounding a single white star.

————

Our state does have a few waterfalls: Tishomingo State Park Falls, Dunn's Falls, Rawson Creek Falls, Seminary Falls, Owen's Creek Falls, and Scutchalo Falls. Most need a good rain to really get cranked up.

————

Mississippi has three international airports. The Jackson-Evers and Gulfport-Biloxi international airports are well-known; the third, however, is the airport at the NASA facility in Hancock County. While there are no international flights to or from Stennis International Airport, it meets the one qualification of an international airport — it houses a U.S. Customs Office.

————

In the northeast corner of Mississippi, Alcorn County is our smallest at 400 square miles. Yazoo County is our largest at 920 square miles. Several counties have ceased to exist. Pearl County dissolved into Marion and Hancock. Bainbridge County was absorbed by Covington in 1824.

————

93% of Mississippians obtain their drinking water from the 18 major aquifers in the state. Only three areas get their municipal drinking supply from surface water systems: Jackson, Tupelo, and communities south of Pickwick Lake.

————

Of our 82 counties, only two — Adams and Jefferson — were formed before 1800. Seven counties were established after 1900. Seven were also named in honor of presidents: Washington, Adams, Jefferson, Madison, Monroe, Lincoln, and Harrison.

————

The mockingbird, Mississippi's state bird, is capable of learning up to 40 distinct sounds. The birds have even been recorded mimicking dogs and sirens.

————

Mississippi females outnumber males 51.6 % to 48.4 %.

————

Per the 2010 Federal Census, the rest of the U.S. has a ration of 87 people to the square mile while Mississippi's is only 63 per square mile.

Alexander Keith McClung, also known as the Black Knight, was perhaps one of Mississippi's most violent and tragic residents. He killed seven male members from one family, in one-on-one firearm duels, after each challenged him for revenge. As the Mississippi 1st Regiment's Lieutenant Colonel, he lost two fingers from his left hand during the Mexican War. A lawyer, editor, and poet, McClung committed suicide at the Eagle Hotel in Jackson in 1855, with his own dueling pistol. The last line of his most famous poem "Invocation to Death" reads "O death, come soon, come soon."

During and after World War II, Mississippi had four primary locations of P.O.W. camps for German and Italian soldiers. The camps were Camp Shelby, Camp Clinton, Camp Como, and Camp McCain. Ten smaller, sub-camps opened in the Delta where prisoners hoed weeds in the fields and picked cotton in the fall. Five sub-camps also opened in the Piney Woods where the prisoners cut trees and replanted seedlings. Prisoners from the camp at Clinton also dug and created the miniature model of the entire Mississippi River. It is still used today by the U.S. Army Corp of Engineers at the Waterways Experiment Station.

Experts estimate a drop of rainfall that falls into the Mississippi River headwater at Lake Itasca, Minnesota reaches the Gulf of Mexico 90 days later. The drop would have traveled 2,352 miles. Minnesota and Louisiana are the only two states through which the river flows. Eight states have the Mississippi River as a border: Mississippi, of course, Arkansas, Tennessee, Kentucky, Missouri, Illinois, Iowa, and Wisconsin.

The small town of Ruleville sports two water towers, standing nearly side-by-side. One is marked "Hot," the other "Cold." The community of Roxie has the last standing wooden water tower in the state.

The major Mississippi filming locations of the Coen Brothers' 2000 hit movie O Brother Where Art Thou? were: Jackson, Valley Park, Oxford, Edwards, Canton, D'Lo, Vicksburg, and Yazoo City.

601 Mississippians in the Navy and Marines were killed in action during World War II. The U.S. Army and Army Air Corps deaths totaled 1,848.

The Neshoba County Fair's tagline "Mississippi's Giant House Party" is a registered trademark.

In the early 1700s France was broke. The king looked to a Scottish financier, John Law, for help. Law devised the Mississippi Company in order to sell shares of stock in the ventures and land speculation in New France. Law did this by issuing paper money (it was a first for France). Easy credit, a rapid upswing in the company's stock price, inflation, and subsequent devaluation of the paper money caused investors to cash out and demand gold and silver in return for their paper. The Mississippi Company became the Mississippi Bubble. The term "millionaire" appeared for the first time during the heyday of the company.

As of late 2011, there were 102 radio stations operating in Mississippi. We have 21 TV stations active now. WJTV (CBS) Jackson is the oldest TV station here, having first telecast in 1953. Laurel's WAML was the state's first radio station, taking the air in 1927, but went silent in 2010.

Senator John McCain's grandfather was from Carroll County. The elder McCain rose to admiral's rank in the Second World War.

The battleship "U.S.S. Mississippi" that was launched in 1904 was decommissioned and sold to Greece in 1914. German bombers sunk her in 1941. The next "U.S.S. Mississippi" battleship was commissioned in 1917 and earned eight battle stars in World War II. Talk of making her a floating museum never came to fruition and she was sold for scrap in 1956.

There are three zoos in Mississippi: Jackson, Hattiesburg, and Tupelo.

Mississippi has one beer brewery located in Kiln. We have one liquor distillery — a vodka-only producer, north of Madison. We have five wineries, located in Natchez, Shubuta, Indianola, Gulfport, and Merigold.

In 2010, 55% of Mississippians lived in rural areas. Ninety years earlier, the 1920 census showed residents' homes as 13% urban and 87% rural.

Mississippi has one nuclear power station, Grand Gulf, outside Port Gibson. In the northeast corner of the state, outside Iuka, sits the empty half-constructed and cancelled station that was to be Yellow Creak Nuclear Power Plant.

With just slightly over 1,400 people, Issaquena is the least populated county in the state. Hinds is the most, with 250,000 persons.

Per the 2010 statistics from the Centers for Disease Control and Prevention, about 23 % of Mississippians use tobacco—either smoking, dipping, or chewing.

————

Mississippi's first execution was in 1818, seven months after statehood. Hanging was the prescribed method and held strong until 1940 when the electric chair arrived. At the time, Mississippi law called for the condemned to be executed in the county of conviction. Mississippi was the only state to ever have a traveling electric chair. The gas chamber took over duties in 1955; then, lethal injection in 2002.

————

Two railroad men were the primary movers and shakers of early Meridian. One wanted to name the settlement Sowashee after the local creek; the other preferred Ragsdale City. They compromised on Meridian, which is neither on nor near a meridian on the globe.

————

It is roughly halfway between the 88th and 89th degree of longitude.

————

The famous Canton Flea Market began in 1965 with local artists hanging their art on the iron fence surrounding the courthouse in the center of the square. It is always held on the second Thursday of May and October.

————

Electric Mills epitomizes the old concept of a company town. The Sumter Lumber Company moved to the spot and had extensive timber holdings for miles around. The company did not buy logs from outside loggers and exclusively cut their own timber. It took 28 years to cut all the trees. They were the first all-electric-powered saw-mill in the country.

————

In Columbus, Tennessee Williams's boyhood home serves as the city's official welcome center.

————

Meridian's Temple Theatre is home to the state's oldest continuously operated theatre or movie palace. It has been in operation since 1927.

————

In the summer of 2012, Central Park hosted the 33rd Annual New York Mississippi Picnic. Beginning in 1979, native Mississippians living in New York began to gather for a party to meet and reacquaint with fellow voluntarily displaced Mississippians. Most other states have followed our lead and created their own Central Park picnics.

In 1915, the King and Queen of the Gypsies of America were traveling near Meridian. The queen died during childbirth and the funeral was held locally. Newspapers reported 20,000 gypsies came from around the nation to attend her final rites.

———

In Tishomingo County, outside Iuka, there is Evergreen Cemetery, but locals call it Toenail Cemetery. The marquee sign even has the alternative name in quotes. As it was being constructed by hand, those trying to create a place of rest lost many a toenail due to the abundance of rocks, roots and stumps on the chosen ground.

———

Fox hunting here arose as sport in the 1920s after the decline of larger game such as deer, panther, and bear. Grenada, Crystal Springs, and Madison are some of the towns with fox hunting clubs.

———

There is a population of white-furred squirrels in Columbia's City Park.

———

In Hancock County in 1961, N.A.S.A. established the Mississippi Test Operation to test rocket motors and engines. After several name changes, it was designated as the Stennis Space Center. The center still tests the engines that power our rockets into outer space.

———

In 1912, an operation called American Pickle Co. based in Wiggins began buying locally grown cucumbers and processing them into pickles. By 1961 it was the largest pickle plant in the entire world. By the late 1970s the locals could not compete with cheaper cucumbers grown in Florida and Mexico. The plant closed in 1980.

———

The town of Madison was born thanks to the railroad and known originally as Madison Station. The growing little town siphoned trade and population away from a nearby separate town on the Natchez Trace known as Madisonville, a town which eventually became extinct. Today Madison is our state's most affluent town with a per capita household income of $60,000, roughly double the state's average.

———

Egg production is big-time Mississippi business. Jackson's Cal-Maine Foods is the largest egg producing company in the entire United States.

———

Ole Miss went coed in 1882 and hired its first female faculty member in 1885.

A source of income for many years in the Piney Woods area has been turpentine production. More than just a paint thinner and remover, turpentine is also used in the production of shoe polish, printing ink, varnish, disinfectants, fireworks, insecticides, crayons, furniture polish, and pharmaceuticals. Turpentine is a byproduct of pine tree resin after it is distilled with other oils.

———

We have six National Forests inside our border: Bienville, Delta, DeSoto, Holly Springs, Homochitto, and Tombigbee.

———

The University of Mississippi acquired its unique and signature moniker—Ole Miss—from an 1897 student's winning entry to name the first yearbook ever published by the school.

———

Four winners of the Miss Mississippi Beauty Pageant have gone on to win the Miss America title: Mary Ann Mobley, Biloxi, 1959; Lynda Lee Mead, Natchez, 1960; Cheryl Prewit, Ackerman, 1980; and Susan Akin, Meridian, 1986.

———

Before the days of income taxes, Northeast Mississippi had a multi-millionaire. Paul J. Rainey, an international playboy, moved to Cotton Plant in Tippah County in 1898 and began buying up huge tracts of land for an animal preserve for his legendary private hunts. The 30,000 acres were stocked with pheasants, wolves, bears, and foxes. That's about 47 square miles of land. His large home even had an indoor heated swimming pool.

———

Mississippi's Hiram Revels is our nation's first African-American congressman. He was seated in the Senate in 1870. An ordained minister, Revels served as chaplain for U.S. Colored Infantry and was present at the Battle of Vicksburg. After his senate term he was succeeded by James L. Alcorn, a political ally. Revels was also the first president of Alcorn State University in Lorman.

———

Before the Civil War, slaves constituted 93% of Issaquena County's population. Today's genealogy hunters use the entire 1860 Federal Census Slave Schedule in their search for ancestors.

———

The author wishes to thank the following organizations, publications and research sites: *The Mississippi Business Journal's Book of Lists*, *Mississippians II* (Nautilus), *Hometown Mississippi* by James F. Brieger, *History of Choctaw, Chickasaw & Natchez* by H.B. Cushman, 1980 Historical and Genealogical Association of Mississippi, Redlands Press, the Mississippi Department of Archives and History, U.S. Census Bureau, University of Mississippi, University of Southern Mississippi, Mississippi State University, Mississippi Public Libraries, the State of Mississippi website ms.gov, the United States Digital Map website, the individual websites of Mississippi counties, and the Sankofagen Wiki website.

ABOUT THE AUTHOR

D.K. White is a fifth-generation Mississippian having been raised in Gulfport, but also having lived in Natchez and Hattiesburg and now resides outside of Jackson. Married for 29 years and proud father of two daughters and a son, White enjoys reading, especially Civil War, Native American and 19th Century histories about the South. He also enjoys researching odd historical facts and winning trivial arguments.